Mind and Self

Also by SUBHASH KAK

The Architecture of Knowledge
The Astronomical Code of the Ṛgveda
The Gods Within
The Nature of Physical Reality
The Prajñā Sūtra: Aphorisms of Intuition
The Wishing Tree
In Search of the Cradle of Civilization
The Aśvamedha

Mind and Self

Patañjali's Yoga Sūtra and Modern Science

Subhash Kak

Mount Meru Publishing

Library and Archives Canada Cataloguing in Publication

Kak, Subhash, 1947-, author

Mind and self : Patañjali's Yoga sūtra and modern science / Subhash Kak.

Includes bibliographical references and index.
Issued in print and electronic formats.
ISBN 978-1-988207-05-6 (paperback).--ISBN 978-1-988207-06-3 (html)

1. Yoga. 2. Patañjali. Yogasūtra. I. Title. II. Title: Patañjali's Yoga sūtra and modern science.

B132 Y6 K34 2016 181'.452 C2016-901981-0
C2016-901982-9

Published in 2016 by:
Mount Meru publishing
P.O. Box 30026
Cityside Postal Outlet PO
Mississauga, Ontario
Canada L4Z 0B6
Email: mountmerupublishing@gmail.com

ISBN 978-1-988207-05-6

Contents

Preface

Yoga is enormously popular around the world although for many it is nothing but the practice of āsanas or physical postures. The āsanas are the first step to deepen the understanding of self since physical practice keeps the body healthy which is essential for the exploration of mind and of inner life. We need to be mindful of our body as the artificial environment of our lives increasingly alienates us from our nature.

Thirty years ago, in *Patañjali and Cognitive Science,* I examined how the understanding of the Yoga-sūtra is validated by several modern insights of neuroscience. I have enlarged my commentary on the Yoga-sūtra and juxtaposed it with newer relevant results from science. Since then I have also written the *Prajñā-Sūtra*, which book complements this one.

Patañjali's text on yoga is from India's early middle period. To get an idea of yoga's earlier history, it is good to consult the Mahābhārata, of which the great yoga classic, the Bhagavad Gītā, is a part. According to the Mahābhārata and the Yājñavalkya Smṛti, Hiraṇyagarbha, which is an epithet for Brahmā, was the original teacher of yoga, and it was the practice of the Vedic way. One can obtain somewhat different insights about the tradition from the Yoga Vāsiṣṭha or the much later Haṭha-Yoga-Pradīpikā, or the many texts of tantra.

I trust in its new incarnation as *Mind and Self,* my commentary will make yoga more accessible both to laypersons as well as scientists and scholars. I am thankful to Liz Swan for her comments on an earlier version of the manuscript.

Subhash Kak
सुभाष चन्द्र काक
Stillwater, Oklahoma

March 9, 2016

Introduction

I. From Mind's Construction of Reality to Yoga

Patañjali's Yoga-sūtra is a systematic exposition on the nature of the mind. It is logical in its method and it questions the naïve understanding of the world. Patañjali takes it that there is a single reality and the multiplicity we see in it is a consequence of the projections of our different minds. Therefore the challenge is to undo the workings of the mind to experience reality in its most directness.

That the mind constructs reality is clearly seen in those who are different from us, especially in persons from a different culture. For example, the witch doctor's death hex on a believer cannot be forestalled by any means. Such voodoo death is brought about by strong emotional shock and fear. But somewhat similar effect of mind on body is seen in modern societies also. There is a medically verified case of a person who was diagnosed with cancer and given just a few months at the end of which he died. But when autopsy was performed it was discovered that the tumor was benign and he was disease-free and the belief in imminent death had been the cause of death.

It is easy enough for us to believe that many people live empty lives but it is much harder for one who has not examined his own life to realize that his life may similarly be seen as empty by others. People of one faith find those of a different faith to hold irrational beliefs. Amongst the non-religious, political beliefs can create insurmountable walls. Reflection on organization of society shows that there is neither perfect order nor perfect laws or justice, and much of how we live is a matter of tradition and convention. Often when people reflect back on earlier phases of their lives, they are surprised at the things that drove them in their youth and bemoan the wasted years.

Mind's constructions of reality are also true of our own culture. The images are strengthened by the media and they become templates for our lives. Our transactions are based on our perceptions of immediate reality and our hopes and fears for the future and, therefore, corporations sell their images to maximize their profits, religious leaders for donations by the people, academics for patronage by funding agencies and the state and politicians for power.

But how could the mind be a problem when this is all we have to experience reality? The problem is that the mind is like a lens which distorts what we see of the world. The kind of distortion produced by this lens depends upon our habits of seeing that are based on inheritance, upbringing, and culture. The way to know ourselves is therefore to know our mind first for it is what gathers and synthesizes our impressions. But since we often conflate ourselves with our minds, it raises many questions related to our individuality.

The idea that the mind is only an instrument and not the true self sets yoga apart from western psychology. Yoga takes up the question of what lies beyond the mind in addition to speaking of its nature, whereas western psychology aims only to describe the many ways the mind works.

It turns out that the way to undo the subjective projections of the mind is to master it and in this process we can dissociate from its workings our personal learnt and unconscious biases. Although this idea appears counterintuitive, scholarly learning creates obstacles for our understanding. Bookish learning does not ask questions about the self. On the other hand, looking within for increasing mastery is fraught with danger for as one enters the labyrinth of the mind, one can get lost in its byways. It is also possible to be so charmed by what one has discovered in one or two rooms of the *house of the mind* that one decides to spend the rest of the life there.

The practice of yoga in the sense of exploring the labyrinth of the mind is *tantra,* and this is why this practice has caused those who are not ethically prepared to use the power they gain by their practice to take advantage of others or get absorbed in sensory pleasures before they have made true progress. Ethical preparation is of the greatest importance in spiritual advancement.

One can speak of two realities: one outer and the other inner. The two should be related since the universe cannot have two ordering principles. If this is so, why do we not in ordinary experience see this unity? This forces us to ask what the personhood of the questioner means.

According to the Vedas, reality *is* and it cannot be described in words. Our conceptions of reality are projections based on habits of the mind, which are generated by saṃskāras or strong impressions. The way forward is to advance our conceptual understanding that depends on our nature and life-experience and slowly reach a deeper experience in which the mind does not act as a filter.

Words fail to completely describe reality because it is the whole, whereas words only address small chunks of it. Reality is interconnected whereas its descriptions capture specific slices of it that lose out on the deeper connections. It is quite like the story of six blind men who felt different parts of an elephant's body to imagine what it looked like. The blind man who feels a leg says it is like a pillar; the one who feels the tail says it is like a rope; the one who feels the trunk says it is like a tree branch; the one who feels the ear says it is like a hand fan; the one who feels the belly says it is like a wall; and the one who feels the tusk says it is like a solid pipe.

How can we go from a naïve view of reality to a deeper understanding? Patañjali says that the artifacts created by the mind's distorting lens should be removed. But how may this be done given that the mind means different things in different settings? It variously means memories, emotions, judgments, dreams, and aspirations. It is easier to speak of its attributes such as perception, reason, imagination, memory, emotion, attention, and a capacity for communication but that doesn't quite tell us what it is. Sometimes we take only the *higher* intellectual functions such as reason and memory to be the actions of the mind but clearly such functions have an emotional basis.

Yoga begins by asserting that its objective is to experience reality directly. But since the mind is the lens through which we see the world, we must first understand the nature of this lens and, paradoxically, this understanding is to be done by the mind. If the mind is the problem, in it are also the instruments for the solution to the problem.

In contrast to the other masterpiece of yoga, the Bhagavad-Gītā, which stresses social aspects of yoga, the Yoga-sūtra is concerned with the individual's personal spiritual journey. Growing up in Kashmir, it was often a part of the conversation amongst adults. This was so partly because my father had studied yoga seriously and spent a few years of discipleship under a master. He had uncommon insight into the nature of the mind and we got glimpses of it in stray remarks by him. One of the remarkable insights he casually mentioned was that the mind assembles stories or narratives that lag behind actual brain processes by a short interval of time, which is an important contemporary discovery in neuroscience.

My father's primary yoga teacher was one Jyoti Prakash Kalia, a lawyer in Reasi in Jammu Province, in whose house my father roomed for a couple of years before he got married. Mr Kalia, who had studied Sri Aurobindo, was a householder and a practicing yogi and he considered himself to belong to Aurobindo's lineage.

Father's apprenticeship with Mr. Kalia provided him unique insights that he was keen to share with family and friends. Since these views ran counter to socialist materialism that the Indian government advocated through the media and school education, father was considered old-fashioned. The community of Kashmiris, like other communities elsewhere in India, became increasingly alienated from its spiritual tradition in the process. Nevertheless, a powerful current of spirituality informed our lives as children. The songs and sayings of mystics such as Lalleśvarī and Rūpa Bhavānī were a part of living culture so it is not surprising that many years later my sister Jaishree chose to write two books on Lalleśvarī. Kashmir had also many living *mad adepts* and my parents never missed a chance to meet them. They had a very close relationship with one yogic master. Orthodox yogis would visit our home from time to time. Father also remained interested in modern masters like Sri Ramakrishna and Aurobindo.

My own study of yoga and the Vedas alternated with intense periods of scientific work. In the earlier seventies I came to know the famous yogi and author Gopi Krishna through his grandson Rakesh Kaul who was a student and friend at Indian Institute of Technology in Delhi. Gopi Krishna was quite in the news then due to his autobiography titled *Kundalini* in which he described astonishing yogic experiences. Later I met many renowned yogis in the United States including Swami Rama who was the first yogi to demonstrate control over the autonomous nervous system.

The conception of the mind in the Yoga-sūtra is the same as that of the Ṛgveda which describes two birds on the tree of which one is eating the fruit and the other merely looks on. This is expressed in the famous metaphor of the chariot in the Kaṭha Upaniṣad and the Bhagavad Gītā. This chariot is the body and its horses are the senses. The immature and unwise person is pulled by the horses; for the wise man it is not the senses that lead the chariot but rather the *witness* within who is detached and liberated and one with the universal self. At first sight the question of two selves itself is perplexing but the *witness* can be taken as the true voice of the self. The unwise person feels he is free but isn't; the wise one appears to have no autonomy, but is free! In the Ṛgvedic image the bird that eats also frets. These two birds are the source of our two voices. For the unwise the two voices are different, but for the wise the two merge into one and it is in this manner that one has transitioned from dual selves to the non-dual self.

In the naïve view, the mind is identical to consciousness and therefore it can be compared to the contents of the brain. In the yogic view, the mind itself is an object although it has elements of subjectivity by virtue of having been modified by its interaction with the universal principle of consciousness (*puruṣa*). As object, the mind is identical to states of the brain.

The yogic view is different from the mind=brain axiom of orthodox neuroscience because it posits another entity that lies beyond the brain. The yogic view acknowledges that from one perspective the mind is just the contents of the brain but as one explores it further one discovers its other characteristics that transcend the brain. In other words, the brain is the doorway to the mind, but it is not the entire story.

The nature of the mind is counterintuitive in the sense that it is simultaneously both the self and separate from it. The premise of the Vedas is that when considered without the modifications that arise due to its association with physical objects, consciousness can provide clues to its own nature. Practices to obtain this knowledge are described in the Vedic books. The Atharvaveda speaks of the community of *vrātyas* who were the yogis of their times.

=========

Although it is common to consider only humans when speaking of mind, nonhuman animals also have wide-ranging cognitive, emotional, and moral capacities. We are neither the only conscious beings nor the sole occupants of the emotional and moral arenas. Animals are conscious for they adapt to ever-changing environments. We know pets to be loyal and affectionate and wild animals have strong emotional bonds in their group and pack. There is overwhelming evidence of the existence of emotions -- some primitive, some complex -- in animals other than humans. Most of the evidence is anecdotal, although there are some examples of controlled studies as well.

These emotions include fear, hope, love, sadness, grief, rage, compassion, shame, aesthetic appreciation, and a sense of justice.

There are sound biological reasons for recognizing animals as conscious beings. There is *evolutionary continuity*, and variations among species are differences in degree rather than kind. We share with other mammals and vertebrates the same areas of the brain that are important for consciousness and processing emotions. The anthropocentric view that only big-brained animals such as humans, nonhuman great apes, elephants, and dolphins and whales have sufficient mental capacities for complex forms of consciousness is incorrect. Human exceptionalism, the belief that human beings have special status based on our unique capacities, is only partly true. We share many traits with other animals.

Philosophical solipsism is often invoked to deny animals consciousness: humans are conscious because we can speak of our awareness whereas dogs and other animals are not conscious because they do not have language. But deaf-mute humans are conscious and, therefore, animals can also be conceivably conscious.

Humans do have unique capacities such as writing poetry, doing abstract mathematics, and meditating on the structure of the universe, but other animals have abilities and traits that we don't possess. Speciesism which justifies cruel treatment of animals based on an assumption of mankind's superiority assigns different values or rights to individuals on the basis of species membership and constructs false boundaries among species. Speciesism is erroneous because it assumes human exceptionalism and also because it ignores within-species variation that often is more marked than between-species differences.

Current knowledge about animal minds does not support the idea of human exceptionalism. It is true that we are a significant force in nature and so we should be compassionate, empathic, and humble and act with great concern for animals and their homes. Each species has a unique place in the scheme of things.

There is a rationale for linking mirror-self recognition to self-awareness. The idea for the experiment came from observations that chimpanzees would, after a period of adjustment, use mirrors to inspect their own images. A widely-replicated protocol that appears to allow a scientific determination of whether it is merely the mirror image *per se* that is the object of interest to the animal inspecting it, or whether it is the image qua proxy for the animal itself that is the object of interest is to take animal subjects and mark their foreheads with a distinctive dye, or, in a control group, only anesthetize them. Upon waking, marked animals who were allowed to see themselves in a mirror touched their own foreheads in the region of the mark significantly more frequently than controls who were either unmarked or not allowed to look into a mirror.

For non-human primates outside the great apes, the evidence for mirror self-recognition has been sparse. Modified versions of this experiment have also been conducted with non-primate species. Various commentators have pointed out that the mirror test may not be entirely fair for species that depend more heavily on senses other than vision.

An intriguing line of research into animals' knowledge of their own mental states considers the performance of animals in situations of cognitive uncertainty. When primates and dolphins are given a *bailout* response allowing them to avoid making difficult discriminations, they choose the bailout option in ways that are very similar to humans. Metacognition, that is awareness of what one knows, comes with a feeling of knowing and animals also appear to possess it.

To speak of an animal at some length, the elephant is like the human in that it needs to learn how to survive in its environment during infancy and adolescence. The lessons learnt include how to feed, use tools and understand complex social structure. The elephant's capacity for memory and emotions is remarkable and is due to the well-developed hippocampus. This is also the area responsible for emotional flashbacks and is the reason that elephants experience post-traumatic stress disorder.

The insight and intelligence of the elephant are particularly noteworthy in the ability to mourn the dead. Recently deceased elephants receive a burial ceremony, while those who are already reduced to a skeleton are paid respect by passing herds. The burial ceremony is marked by deep rumblings while the dead body is touched and caressed by the herd members' trunks.

Intelligence is also manifested in the elephant's ability to self-medicate. When a pregnant mother is due to give birth, she will chew on the leaves of a certain tree to induce labor.

Another ability that indicates superior intellect is the elephant's ability to play, mimic sounds, and display a sense of humor. Games include throwing a stick at a certain object, passing an object from one animal to another, or squirting water out of the trunk in a fountain. Elephants in zoos have even been seen stealing onlookers' caps and hiding them in playful teasing.

Elephants have been observed digging holes for drinking water, then molding bark from a tree into the shape of a ball and placing it on top of the hole and covering it over with sand to avoid evaporation. They also use sticks to scratch their backs where their trunk cannot reach. Elephants recognize themselves in a mirror.

Here's a personal account of a pet parakeet that lived with us to 11 years of age. She lived in our house with another bird, a cockatiel, in cage and outside. Unlike the cockatiel, which was very social, the parakeet kept aloof after her failed early attempts to socialize with the cockatiel. She never came to us of her own volition until one day she hopped out of her cage (both the birds had free play inside the house) and walked over to my wife and I in the living room. She walked up our legs and let her be stroked for several minutes by both of us. The next day she died. It is as if she had a premonition of death and she wished to say goodbye to us.

=========

Animals are *sufficiently* intelligent because they survive in their ecological environment. Even in cognitive tasks of the kind normally associated with human intelligence, animals perform well. Thus rats might find their way through a maze, or dolphins may solve logical problems involving some kind of generalization. These performances could, in principle, be used to define a gradation.

The tasks that set the human apart from the machine are those that relate to abstract conceptualization best represented by language understanding. But nobody will deny that deaf-mutes, who don't have a language, do think. Language is best understood as a subset of a large repertoire of behavior.

Examples of animal intelligence include mynah birds who can recognize trees or people in pictures, and signal their identification by vocal utterances -- words -- instead of pecking at buttons, and a parrot who can answer, vocally, questions about shapes and colors of objects, even those not seen before. The intelligence of higher animals, such as apes, elephants, and dolphins is even more remarkable.

Animal intelligence experiments suggest that one can speak of different styles of solving intelligence problems. Are the cognitive capabilities of nonhuman animals limited because their style has fundamental limitations? Their relatively low scores on some tests may be explained on the unnatural conditions in which the experiments are performed. Nevertheless, at certain tasks the intelligence shown by nonhuman animals remains beyond the capability of machines.

Animal behavior has a recursive nature, or part-whole hierarchy. Considering this from the bottom up, animal societies are superorganisms. For example, the ants in an ant colony are like cells, their castes like tissues and organs, the queen and her drones like the generative system, and the exchange of liquid food amongst the colony members like the circulation of blood and lymph. Furthermore, corresponding to morphogenesis in organisms the ant colony has sociogenesis, which consists of the processes by which the individuals undergo changes in caste and behavior. Such recursion exists all the way up to the earth itself seen as a living entity, somewhat like the unconscious brain. Paralleling this recursion is the individual who is a collection of several *agents* with their corresponding sub-agents which are the sensory mechanisms. These agents are bound together and this binding is a characteristic of consciousness.

The processing by the brain has several components that include association, self-organization, and recognition of wholes. Associative neural learning proceeds to create necessary structures to "measure" the stimulus-space; at the higher level of multiple agents the response is by reorganizing the grosser levels of the neural structure. Each cognitive agent is an abstract quantum system. The linkages amongst the agents are regulated by an appropriate quantum field. This allows the individual at the higher levels of abstraction to initiate cognition or action, leading to active behavior.

That cognitive ability cannot be viewed simply as a processing of sensory information by a central intelligence extraction system is confirmed by individuals with anomalous abilities. Savants perform spectacularly at certain tasks. Anomalous performance has been noted in the areas of mathematical and calendar calculations; music; art, including painting, drawing or sculpting; mechanical ability; prodigious memory (mnemonism); unusual sensory discrimination or *extrasensory* perception. These abilities cannot be understood in the framework of computer-type mind.

Since the material world is not causally closed, and consciousness influences its evolution, body and mind complement each other. At the level of the individual, even medical science that is strongly based on the machine paradigm is acknowledging the influence of mind on body.

=========

Many years ago, I proposed the term *quantum neural computing* to suggest that the complete neural system of an organism defines a whole and it can be viewed as a quantum system at its deepest level and a classical system at the embodied level. Whereas its neural connections constitute the conscious system which is classical, the quantum system is supported by the virtual particles associated with its dynamic states. The philosophical idea behind this proposal was that like material objects abstract entities also have a reality that is subject to quantum laws. This proposal was not to suggest that the brain's structures supported quantum coherent processes in the network of neurons but rather that the brain's functioning as a whole was according to quantum laws at a deeper level.

A quantum system underlying brain structures cannot explain intentionality, group dynamics, and other peculiarities of sentient behavior. The fact that subjective conscious states can remain "coherent" across different individuals who are separated across space and time (as in coordinated social behavior) indicates that these states are related to a universal function. There is a dialog between this function and the neural processes inside the brain but it is not one-sided and it can embrace many individuals.

At the atomic level nature follows quantum laws. These laws are different from classical laws in two important respects. First, a quantum system is a superposition of mutually exclusive attributes; second, when a measurement is made on the quantum system only one of its constituent attributes will be registered by the measurement device. In contrast, a classical object has well defined attributes that can be measured with precision.

The photon, a particle-like representation of light quantum, can thus be in a superposition of horizontally and vertically polarized photons. If the measurement can be only in these two bases, what will be registered for an incoming photon (which may be in a superposition) will be either of these two constituent states. There exist some macroscopic quantum states also but neuroscientists believe that the states of the brain are not quantum.

The superposition of mutually exclusive attributes and the collapse of the state function have the most astonishing philosophical and operational implications. The same kind of object behaves differently in different situations. Two or many very distantly located objects can be so entangled that if a measurement collapses the state function on one particle, the state function of the other remotely situated particle will also collapse in the same manner. This entanglement property suggests that there is a deeper order in the universe.

In the mid-nineties, Karl Pribram invited me to participate in a conference on Learning as Self-Organization for which he had brought together leading neuroscientists and where my role as an outsider to that group was to give a broader systems perspective on the problem. I chose the title "The three languages of the brain: quantum, reorganizational, and associative" where I argued that in addition to self-organization, one must also consider associational and quantum aspects of learning.

The associative and reorganizational languages are quite apparent from experimental findings; it is much harder to establish conclusively that the brain exhibits quantum properties.

Several modes of expression characterize living systems whereas non-living systems have only one mode of expression. A non-living system, no matter how complex, can, in principle, be described fully in terms of its response to different interactions whereas a living system cannot because of its adaptability and agency. A living system uses several languages because its behavior is active and it is associated with attention. This sets up a duality since selectively concentrating on a part of the environment implies ignoring other parts.

Whereas one can determine whether a *small* system is operating according to quantum laws by experiments related to superposition of the relevant states and obtaining of outcomes in a *probabilistic* fashion upon interaction with the system, the situation with a *large* system, whose structure is accessible to experimentation, is more troublesome. In small systems such as a proton, the internal structure in terms of quarks is not taken into consideration in accounting its behavior as a quantum object, but there is no reason why one should not ask as to what happens to the internal structure in an interaction. Since the structure of the large system is accessible in principle, one needs a consistent narrative to explain the specific output.

It appears that a generalization of the complementary principle is needed to deal with the behavior of *large* quantum systems. The concept of complementarity is used to imbed quantum mechanics in a coherent and rational framework. Since the final representation of observations is in our sense experience that is described in classical terms, there is a logical incompatibility between the quantum process and its observation. According to complementarity, a process may be explained as a particle picture or a wave picture, but not both, simultaneously.

Biological organisms exhibit individuality, and, therefore, their behavior may be either seen as a consequence of effort, will, and intention or a learnt response which are complementary pictures. Neither of these views is sufficient to explain all behavior and thus the situation is analogous to that of duality of quantum theory. A large quantum system may be seen, by an extension of the idea of complementarity, either as responding in a random fashion to a stimulus when seen as a unity, or as reorganizing itself so that the behavior can be accounted for in the reorganized structure.

Self-organization is a characteristic of complex systems. Such systems are associated with a few stable states. As the system conditions change, the state either stays in its initial stable state or transitions to another stable state.

The brain is a self-organizing system which responds to the nature and quality of its interaction with the environment. Other ecological systems, which are biological communities that have complex interrelationships amongst their components, are self-organizing, without being self-aware. This suggests that while self-organization is necessary for consciousness, it is not sufficient.

Cognitive scientists have considered evolutionary aspects related to cognitive capacity, where consciousness is viewed as emerging out of language. Linguistic research on chimpanzees and bonobos has revealed that although they can be taught basic vocabulary of several hundred words, this linguistic ability does not extend to syntax. By contrast, small children acquire much larger vocabularies -- and use the words far more creatively -- with no overt training, suggesting that language is an innate capacity.

According to the nativist view, language ability is rooted in the biology of the brain, and our ability to use grammar and syntax is an instinct, dependent on specific modules of the brain. We learn language as a consequence of unique biological adaptation, and not because it is an emergent response to the problem of communication confronted by ourselves and our ancestors.

It is believed that human language capacities arose out of biological natural selection because they fulfill two clear criteria: an extremely complex and rich design and the absence of alternative processes capable of explaining such complexity. Other theories look at music and language arising out of sexual selection. But, howsoever imaginative and suggestive these models might be, they do not address the question of how the capacity to visualize models of world that are essential to language and consciousness first arises.

There is a philosophical critique of the search for a theory of consciousness. According to this critique, all that *normal* science can hope to achieve is a description of objects. But consciousness is a property of the subject, the experiencing "I", which, owing to its nature, forever lies outside the pale of *normal* science. The experimenter cannot turn his gaze upon himself, and ordinary reality must have a dual aspect. This duality means that the world of objective causality is incomplete, creating a fundamental paradox: If objects are described by normal science, why is it that science is not rich enough to describe the psychological body associated with the experiencing subject?

=========

In blindsight, people who are perceptually blind in a certain area of their visual field demonstrate some response to visual stimuli. In one type, these subjects, who have no awareness whatsoever of any stimuli, are able to predict, at levels significantly above chance, aspects of a visual stimulus, such as location, or type of movement, often in a forced-response or guessing situation.

In anosognosia, a person who suffers a dramatic disability, such as blindness or paralysis, seems unaware of it. It can be selective in that the affected person with multiple impairments may seem unaware of only one handicap, while appearing to be fully aware of any others. Those diagnosed with dementia of the Alzheimer's type often display this lack of awareness and insist that nothing is wrong with them.

A phantom limb is the feeling that an amputated or missing limb (even an organ, like the appendix) is still attached to the body and is moving appropriately with other body parts. Many amputees experience painful phantom sensations in their amputated limb. Phantom limb pain is intermittent and the frequency and intensity of attacks usually decline with time. A slightly different sensation known as phantom pain can also occur in people who are born without limbs and people who are paralyzed.

Intuition may be seen as akin to blindsight. Strong unconscious urges can similarly be seen as arising from the body and mind seeking completion.

There are people with mental disorders who wish to have a perfectly good leg amputated or some others who think they have three arms, when they clearly do not. These bizarre conditions - named body integrity identity disorder (BIID) and supernumerary phantom limb, respectively - have a neurological basis. These conditions occur as a result of abnormal activity in a part of the brain which is known to be involved in constructing a mental representation of the body, or body image.

Medical findings suggest BIID occurs as a result of abnormal activity in the right parietal lobe, which is known to be essential for constructing a mental representation of the body. Specifically, this body image is constructed in the superior parietal lobule (SPL), which performs a function referred to as multisensory integration, whereby different types of sensory information entering the brain are brought together. Thus, information from the visual parts of the brain and the primary somatosensory cortex, which processes tactile sensations and proprioceptive information relating to the position of the body within space, is sent to the superior parietal lobule. There, it is combined with information from the motor cortex, which controls movement, and all is processed further to generate an internal model of the body.

BIID arises as a result of abnormal function in the right parietal lobe when the brain does not register the limb as a part of the body, and contains no representation of it, so it is not incorporated into the body image. As a result, the subject has no sense of ownership over the limb, and feels strongly that it does not belong to him. It feels extraneous or redundant, so he wishes to have it removed.

Supernumerary phantom limb is a much rarer condition, in which the patient experiences the presence of an extra limb, usually following a stroke. Mostly this feels much the same as the phantom limbs of amputees - an illusion, from which sensations sometimes emanate. But in a small number of cases the patients report that they can also see the limb, and some even say that they can feel and use it. The patient's brain has generated a virtual simulation of a fully functional arm, which has been incorporated into the body image.

This is consistent with the view that the brain constructs a mental representation of the body by integrating different types of sensory information. In the case of supernumerary phantom limb, the distortion is obviously acquired - it occurs as the result of a stroke. The parts of the brain which relay body image-related sensory information to the SPL have been starved of oxygen due to cell death. This perturbs SPL function, and so distorts the body image. In this case, the brain's representation of the left arm has been duplicated, and incorporated into the mental scheme of the body.

In BIID, the situation is apparently reversed: the body image is missing a representation of the affected limb. The body image distortion seen in BIID is congenital. Children born with missing arms or legs sometimes experience phantom limb syndrome, suggesting that there is a representation of the non-existent limb in the brain.

II. Outer and Inner Skies

As children we first negotiate our place in the outer world by making sense of our identity personally and socially. At that time we don't question our nature because most of the time we are concerned with our physical safety and comfort. Later, when we have occasion to turn our gaze inwards we realize that our place in the outer sky is made familiar to us by our replay of it on the inner sky.

Mainstream science tells us that our behavior is driven fundamentally by instincts that encapsulate our evolutionary experience quite like that of other animals. The difference between us and animals is advanced language that gives us the capacity to reflect. But language doesn't seem to provide answers related to our deepest self and at some point we ask why the understanding of the outer world is even possible.

Socially, one lives in two somewhat overlapping circles: one determined by morality and law; and the other determined by one's notions of self. One may choose to live according to the expectations of one's familial and social group, do one's duties, and be a good citizen without worrying about larger questions of meaning. Or one may ask who one is beyond one's name and history and wonder why one likes certain things and doesn't like other things. The first circle is the domain of Viṣṇu, and the second is that of Śiva. If Viṣṇu is the deity of morality, friendship, and devotion, Śiva is the deity of consciousness, of the being within who is hidden in one's deepest self.

Outwardly, being on the path of Viṣṇu appears relatively easy and that of Śiva to be painful. People pick one or the other path based on their innate temperament. The path of inward search first reveals several selves within. At a more philosophical level, in the transitions between these selves, the individual dies many deaths and is reborn. This is the dance of Śiva that destroys and creates at each moment and at many levels.

We can also see the universe, at the outer or the inner levels, from the perspective of time. Outwardly, it is the problem of whether the universe is being or becoming, or both. Inwardly, it is time in its embodiment as change which is the domain of the Goddess. Psychologically and emotionally, it is surrender to this change that brings comfort.

Standard outer science is the search for universal principles that describe material processes. Yoga is the striving to get connected to the universal self. This self is necessitated by logic as the body by itself cannot be the experiencer and it can only be the contents of the experience.

The outer and the inner worlds are connected as the outer, at one level, is merely the contents of the inner. In other words, the exploration of the outer is also the exploration of the inner. The fact that we can even make sense of the outer world is due to the connections between the outer and the inner. The Vedic texts speak of the connections repeatedly and they are called *bandhu*. Ancient mythologies acknowledge these connections: the gods and the demons reside in the sky and also in the firmament of our inner space.

Amongst the *bandhus* described in the Vedic texts are the processes in the body that are attuned to astronomical periods. These biological clocks exist in all cells and they are a part of mainstream science. The Puruṣa Sūkta of the Ṛgveda speaks thus of the eye and the mind to be in consonance with the periods of the sun and the moon, which has been confirmed by the science of biological cycles. Other terrestrial processes are tuned to the tides or the motion of the plane of the moon.

Living organisms have rhythms that correspond to the periods of the sun, the moon, and the planets. The potato has a variation in its metabolic processes that is matched to the sidereal day, the 23-hour 56-minute period of rotation of the earth relative to the fixed stars. Biological clocks are precise and they are tuned to different periods such as 24 hours (according to the day), 24 hours and 50 minutes (according to the lunar day since the moon rises roughly 50 minutes later every day) or its half representing the tides, 29.5 days (the period from one new moon to the next), and the year. Monthly rhythms, averaging 29.5 days, are reflected in the reproductive cycles of many organisms. In humans the menstrual period corresponds to the moon's motion; in fact *menses* means lunar month.

A unique deep-sea lily (echinoderm) near Japan liberates its sex cells once every year in October at about 3 PM on the day of one of the moon's quarters. In succeeding years the time of sex cell release changes, among the moon's two quarters, first-third-first, to progressively slightly earlier dates in October. The triplets are repeated until about the first of the month whereupon the following year it jumps abruptly to near the end of the month to start the advancing triplet progression again. The result is an 18-year cycle, which is essentially the period of regression of the Moon's orbital plane.

The gestation periods for mammals must have provided the basis for singling out certain animals as special symbols. Some of these periods are:

ass	365 days
sacred baboon	183 days
lion	108 days
cow	280 days
dog	61 days
goat	151 days
sheep	147 days
horse	337 days
human	280 days

It is no surprise then that the ass is used as a symbol for the year in the Śatapatha Brāhmaṇa. The horse with its average gestation period only one day off from the nakṣatra year of 336 days (for 28 nakṣatras) is a natural symbol for the year in the context of the nakṣatras. The gestation period of the sacred baboon is exactly half of the solar year, and this is likely to have played a role in the special significance attached to it by the Egyptians. That the gestation periods for the human and the cow are identical is one reason for the sacredness assigned to the cow.

The yoga books speak of three skies which are the physical sky (*bhautika ākāśa* or *bhūtākāśa*), the sky of the mind (*citta ākāśa*), and the sky of consciousness (*cid ākāśa*). Of these, the sky of consciousness is the most subtle and powerful and it is this that engenders the connections with the other two skies. The sky of the mind is not fully illumined and its darkness causes the individual to think that the physical sky is the primary reality. When the light of consciousness shines in the sky of the mind, then the individual becomes enlightened.

The twentieth century sage Ramaṇa Maharṣi described the three skies thus: "The natural state is cidākāśa; the I feeling that is born from cidākāśa is cittākāśa. As that cittākāśa expands and takes the shape of the bhūtas (elements), it is called bhūtākāśa. When the cittākāśa which is consciousness of the self does not see the cidākāśa but sees the bhūtākāśa, it is said to be mano ākāśa and when it leaves mano ākāśa and sees cidākāśa it is said to be *cinmaya* (pure consciousness). The subsiding of the mind means that the idea of multiplicity of objects vanishes and the idea of oneness of objects appears. When that is achieved, everything appears natural."

Yogic practices make the individual aware of the three skies and the relationship between their contents. More importantly, they help the individual to erase invalid links that they have imposed on the three which resulted in their confusion about the nature of reality.

In the Prajñā-Sūtra, the essence of the Vedic system is described as the categories *bandhu*, *parokṣa* (paradox), and *yajña* (sacrifice) that leads to transformation. Yoga is what happens when yajña is done. This yajña need not only be outer and physical; it is more often internal. The āsanas and other limbs of yoga are elements of an inner yajña.

An important implication of bandhus is that the inner objects have characteristics quite similar to the outer ones. Just as one needs exercise for the body, one needs so for the inner body. The inner body can become flabby and diseased. It is harder for one to know the condition of the inner body because there is no easy way to see oneself in the mind-mirror. Many of the steps of Patañjali's yoga are to exercise the inner body.

The idea of recursion is at the basis of the connections between the outer and the inner skies. This recursion, as detailed in the Prajñā–Sūtra, is the repetition of patterns to different scales and across time. These are patterns not only of materiality but also of ideas. Perhaps the most dramatic acknowledgement of such recursion is the centrality of the number 108 in the Indian tradition. This number, which is approximately the distance in Sun and Moon diameters of the Sun and the Moon from the earth, as well as the diameter of the Sun in terms of the Earth diameters, was taken as a measure of the inner space of the individual. For this reason, many spiritual practices were done 108 times. In the sacred geography of India that characterizes the location of its great temples, the number 108 has a prominent place.

=========

Reductionism takes brain and mind to be identical, with mind as the sum total of the activity in the brain viewed at a suitable higher level of representation. Opposed to this is the viewpoint that although mind requires a physical structure, it transcends that structure.

The mind processes signals coming into the brain to obtain its understandings in the domains of seeing, hearing, touching, and tasting using its store of memories. But a cognitive act is an active process where the selectivity of the sensors and the accompanying processing in the brain is organized based on the expectation of the cognitive task and on effort, will and intention. Intelligence is a result of the workings of numerous active cognitive agents yet it is more than a sum of its parts as evidenced most strikingly by the capabilities of savants and accounts of the creative moment.

Memory plays a large role in the explanation of the workings of the mind in the Yoga-sūtra. But memory itself has much variety. We know that when we store a memory, we are storing information. It is the nature of the information that determines how long it is retained and how it is retained. There is also the question of what exactly is stored since what is recalled is never exactly what the senses took in at the moment of experience. The mind takes the sensory input and then constructs the memory.

Very broadly, there are two categories of memory: *short-term memory* (or working memory) and *long-term memory*, based on the amount of time it is stored. Both can weaken due to age or a variety of other reasons, such as trauma or stroke. Long-term memory is the brain's system for storing, managing, and retrieving information. Short-term memory or working memory does its functions in the mind before either being dismissed or transferred to long-term memory.

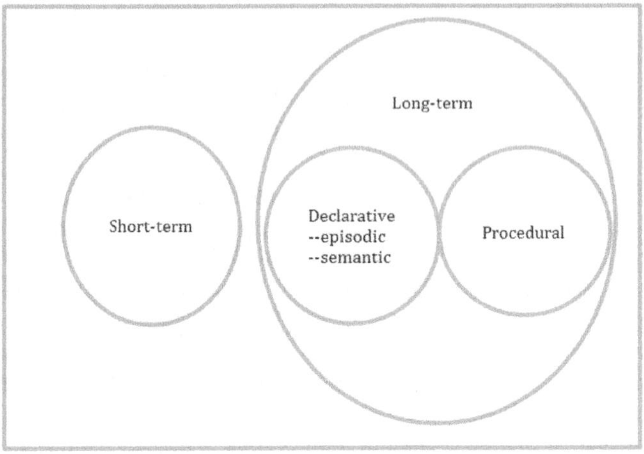

Kinds of memory

Long-term memories are much more complex than short-term ones. Different types of information (such as procedures, life experiences, and language) are stored with separate memory systems. *Explicit memory*, or declarative memory, is a type of long-term memory, which requires conscious thought. It's this that is normally meant by memory when judgment about somebody's memory being good or bad is made. Explicit memory is often associative in a manner that links different categories together.

Declarative memory is flexible and can be readily applied to novel situations, while non-declarative memory tends to be inflexible and defined in the context of the learning situation. Implicit knowledge is not readily accessed by response systems that did not participate in the original learning.

Episodic memory is one type of explicit memory. It is autobiographical and it provides the individual with record of personal experiences. This memory makes it possible for one to remember specific sequence of events of life. Its quality depends on its emotional content. This form of memory appears to be centered in the brain's hippocampus—with considerable help from the cerebral cortex.

Another type of explicit memory is *semantic memory.* It accounts for our *textbook learning* or general knowledge about the world. It enables us to say, without knowing exactly when and where we learned, that a zebra is a striped animal, or that Washington is the capital city of the United States. We don't know where semantic memory is stored in the brain; some say in the hippocampus and related areas, while others think it's widely spread throughout the brain. As with episodic memory, semantic memory ranges from strong (recall) to weak (familiarity). Unlike episodic memory, semantic memory is better sustained over time.

From the moment of birth, the individual is exposed to a world full of sensations and information. These experiences have the potential to end up as autobiographical memories that involve both episodic and semantic memories.

Implicit memory (or *non-declarative memory*) is another major form of long-term memory that does not require conscious thought. It allows one to do things by rote. This memory isn't always easy to verbalize, since it flows effortlessly in our actions. Implicit memory lets us recall and make judgments about words, objects, and images without any conscious recall of prior experience. That is, we have an aspect of memory that is not a component of conscious recall. Consequently, we cannot view memory as something that is stored somewhere. Rather, we need to see it as part of the brain's reorganization process.

Procedural memory is one type of implicit memory that makes it possible for us to carry out commonly learned tasks without consciously thinking about them. Riding a bike, tying shoelaces, and washing dishes are tasks that require procedural memory. Even natural tasks, such as walking, require procedural memory. The tasks associated with procedural memory are done easily, but it is hard to verbalize exactly how they are done.

Procedural memory likely uses a different part of the brain than episodic memory. Brain injury can cause the loss of specific procedural memories. The amnesic often retains procedural memory: how to use a fork or drive a car, for example. On the other hand, a person can lose the capacity to read, but still be able to write. Procedural memory is also associated with saṃskāras. Much of normal human action is repeated play of procedural memory.

Priming is increased sensitivity to certain stimuli due to prior experience. Because priming it believed to occur outside of conscious awareness, it is different from memory that relies on the direct retrieval of information. Direct retrieval utilizes explicit memory, while priming relies on implicit memory. Research has also shown that priming can affect the decision-making process. We are primed by experiences; if something was heard very recently, or many more times than another thing, one is primed to recall it more quickly. This *priming* phenomenon operates across a wide range of sensory and motor systems, at various levels of processing. Implicit memory is a manifestation of priming.

An example of priming is that the smell of the freshly baked bread when walking into a store makes one more likely to buy some bread. Priming also applies to motor skills, physical exertion, intellectual capacity, and social graces. If a person reads a list of words including the word *table*, and is later asked to complete a word starting with *tab*, the probability that he or she will answer *table* is greater than if not so primed.

Another example of positive priming involves showing a subject an incomplete picture which they cannot identify. More pieces of the picture are shown until the picture is recognized. If the same test is done many weeks later, the subject will identify the picture far quicker than they did first time around. It is believed that spreading activation is responsible for the effects of priming.

The central executive is an attentional system that controls various visual and auditory subsystems, relating them to long-term memory. One auditory system is the *phonological loop*, which involves some process of rehearsal with subvocal speech to maintain the memory trace. Likewise, there appears to be a visio-spatial sketchpad that helps us memorize images.

The ability to remember depends on mood and the level of physiological arousal. Performance appears to improve as arousal increases, up to some peak, beyond which it deteriorates. Different tasks are optimally performed at different levels of arousal. Memories are also lost with time. Although learning appears to be linearly related to time, forgetting has a logarithmic relationship: the information loss is very rapid at first, and then it slowly levels off.

Short-term retention is influenced by events experienced during the retention interval (*retroactive interference*) and those occurring prior to the event that is to be remembered (*proactive interference*). Retroactive interference involves memory impairment caused by events between learning and testing—a new memory can supersede or otherwise impact an older one. In *proactive inhibition*, the reverse process occurs: an old memory interferes with our ability to learn new information. The interplay of these categories is at the basis of the unique characteristics of the cognitive system.

Many kinds of sensory memory systems help us perceive the world. For example, visual memory includes components that let a memory trace persist for about one-tenth of a second. This persistence lets us see continuous motion in the discrete frames of a television broadcast. Another component to this memory, more sensitive to shape than brightness, integrates information arriving from the two retinas. Like visual persistence, a memory related to auditory persistence creates an echo that lingers after the item has been spoken. That's why we remember the later words in a series better if we hear them rather than read them.

There are memories about facts, events, skills, and habits as well. Some are based on language, others aren't. Fact and event memory is distinct from other kinds of memory, such as the memory forming the basis of skills and habits. Declarative memory dealing with facts and events can be in chunks as small as single events. Although we generally acquire non-declarative memory across several presentations of the stimulus, in situations such as taste aversion, a person might acquire it after a single event.

In perceptual representational learning, the experience of an object on one occasion facilitates the perception of the same or a similar object on a subsequent occasion. If semantic memory represents the individual's general knowledge of the world, episodic memory structures our personal experiences. Semantic memory includes the meaning of words, formulas of different kinds, and geographical knowledge, whereas episodic memory deals with particular incidents, such as a visit to the doctor last week. If we consider the distinction between short- and long-term memories, we note that in human amnesia, short-term memory is usually intact. The problem therefore relates to the storage of the information and not impairment in perception or rule learning.

=========

The brain has several modules each of which is essentially an autonomous neural network. Thus the visual network responds to visual stimulation and also to visual imagery and the motor network produces movement and it is active during imagined movements. At the same time the brain has a higher integrative or interpretive module that synthesizes the actions of the lower modules. Such a logical structure leads to several paradoxes which can be viewed as being similar to paradoxes of logic and physics.

The Fourier approach to sensory perception is the basis for my friend Karl Pribram's holonomic theory of brain function. Holonomy, as its name implies, is related to the unconstrained Fourier co-ordinate system described by holography. The Fourier transformation changes a space-time coordinate system into a spectral coordinate system within which the properties of our ordinary images are spread throughout the system.

Taking the visual system as an example, the form of an optical image is transformed by the retina into a quantum process that is transmitted to the visual cortex. Each dendritic receptive field thus represents the spread of the properties of that form originating from the entire retina. Taken together, cortical receptive fields form patches of dendritic local field potentials and the spread of properties occurs within each patch and there is no spread of the Fourier process over the large extent of the entire cortex. In order to serve the perceptual process the patches must become assembled by the operation of nerve impulses in axonal circuits. The processing of the vibratory sensory inputs in audition and in tactile sensation proceeds somewhat similarly.

III. Patañjali and His Times

According to tradition Patañjali was an expert on yoga, grammar, and Āyurveda and the author of the Yoga-sūtra, Mahābhāṣya, and the Nidānasūtra. He spent time in Pāṭaliputra (modern Patna), the capital of the then Indian Empire, and achieved fame there.

There is evidence supporting the view that Patañjali, the author of the grammar Mahābhāṣya was from Kashmir. The scholar Ashok Aklujkar has provided a series of arguments in support of this view. These include that Patañjali's descriptions of the geography of northwest India is detailed unlike that of other regions.

The current manuscripts of the Mahābhāṣya go back to one written in Kashmir and the acquaintance of Kashmirian scholars with this text was of high order and its study was patronized by Kashmirian kings.

Other reasons in favor of this identification include the fact that Patañjali is considered the reincarnation of Śeṣanāga or Ananta, the great snake on whose back Viṣṇu lies during the cessation of the universe. Ananta is credited in the Nīlamata Purāṇa with the draining of the valley of Kashmir thus making it habitable. Kashmir is associated with the worship of snakes or *nāgas*. Aklujkar believes that the myth of Patañjali's birth in the hands of a woman standing in water supports the case of Kashmir. The great Kārkoṭa Dynasty of Kashmir is also associated with the origin from a nāga.

A royal sacrifice done at the behest of the Śuṅga Emperor Puṣyamitra is described in the Mahābhāṣya and Patañjali may very well have attended it. Puṣyamitra (died 151 BCE, r. 185–151 BCE) was the founder and first King of the Śuṅga dynasty. Originally a *senāpati* (general) he killed the last Mauryan Emperor Bṛhadratha during an army review, and proclaimed himself King. He then performed the Aśvamedha yajña and brought much of Northern India under his rule.

Not all modern scholars consider the Patañjali of the texts on yoga and grammar and the Patañjali of Āyurveda to be the same person. In any case, the discipline of yoga is very old and there is evidence that it was practiced during the Harappan tradition that began around 8000 BCE. The five thousand year Paśupati seal that shows a person in a yogic posture is proof of its existence in the Harappan tradition.

There are many descriptions of yoga in the Mahābhārata which is by all accounts anterior to Patañjali. In this book, the sage Vasiṣtha speaks of yoga as *ekāgratā*, one pointed concentration, and Bhīṣma instructs Yudhiṣṭhira in four stages of *dhyāna-yoga.* The Bhagavad Gītā speaks of four kinds of yoga: *karma-yoga*, the path of action, *jñāna-yoga*, the path of knowledge, *bhakti-yoga*, the path of devotion, and *dhyāna-yoga*, the path of meditation. The Kaṭha and the Śvetāśvatara Upaniṣads speak of yoga directly. In the Kaṭha Upaniṣad it is Yama (Death) who teaches the science of yoga to the seeker Naciketas; in the Śvetāśvatara Upaniṣad it is told that one should control the mind and practice yoga which would release the subject from bondage.

In the Maitrī Upaniṣad, it is said that yoga has six *aṅgas* or limbs which are listed as *prāṇāyāma*, breath control, *pratyāhāra,* sense-withdrawal, *dhyāna*, meditation, *tarka*, logic, and *samādhi*, absorption. Five of these limbs are also found in Patañjali's scheme.

The oldest and the best-known commentary on the Yoga-sūtra is the Yoga-Bhāṣya by Vyāsa (believed to have lived in 4th century CE). Other important commentaries were written by Vācaspati Miśra (9th century), King Bhoja (10th century) and Vijñānabhikṣu (15th century). In the past century innumerable translations and commentaries have appeared as the popularity of Yoga has soared around the world.

Although the Yoga-sūtra is popular and read widely, it is interpreted in diverse ways. Many people think that the purpose of yoga is to develop extraordinary powers within oneself. But how is that possible if the world unfolds according to physical law? One may also ask: What is the source of intuition, freedom and creativity?

According to Patañjali, the commonality of our experience of the physical world validates its objective existence. He also claims that the physical reality has a unity; its different forms are a result of transformations that vary the balance of its primary constituents. This is quite like the philosophy of modern science excepting that modern science does not accept any principle that transcends material reality.

The metaphor used to describe the nature of consciousness is that of a jewel within a cover. The everyday consciousness that equates itself with the body is ripples on this cover, but it is not explained why this consciousness *forgets* its true nature. Patañjali takes the mind to have a hierarchical structure. The everyday consciousness forms associations of the external reality, whereas the inner self acts as the witness. The spectrum of the different states of mind is the various states between these two extremes.

IV. Paradoxical Knowledge and the Veda

Perhaps the first grand synthesis of the dichotomous logics of the inanimate and the living worlds is to be found in the hymns of the Ṛgveda. The principal idea of these hymns is that reality is paradoxical if analyzed by the categories of time, space, matter, and mind. The Vedic sages argued that since one relates to the universe through the mind, the key to the resolution of these paradoxes is in the understanding of the nature of consciousness. Meditation became the way to knowledge. The Vedic sages asserted that the mind could, through discipline, be trained to transcend its ordinary limitations to apprehend the non-dichotomous reality underlying the everyday reality of our ordinary senses.

According to the Vedic view, reality, which is unitary at the transcendental level, is projected into experience which is characterized by duality and paradox. We thus have duality associated with body and consciousness, being and becoming, greed and altruism, fate and freedom. The Gods bridge such duality in the field of imagination and also collectively in society: Viṣṇu is the deity of moral law, whereas Śiva is Universal Consciousness. Conversely, the projection into processes of time and change is through the agency of the Goddess. Consciousness (*puruṣa*) and Nature (*prakṛti*) are opposite sides of the same coin.

The Vedic view must be contrasted from Indian materialism that viewed consciousness as arising out of the complexity of the body. The school called Cārvāka or Lokāyata has been traced to around 600 BCE in the teachings of one Bṛhaspati. Quite like the modern materialist, the Cārvākas believe only the physical world. Knowledge is merely a record of perceptions, and any reasoning going beyond sense experience is invalid. Since one can only perceive particulars and not universals, inference, which must include a universal connection, is impossible.

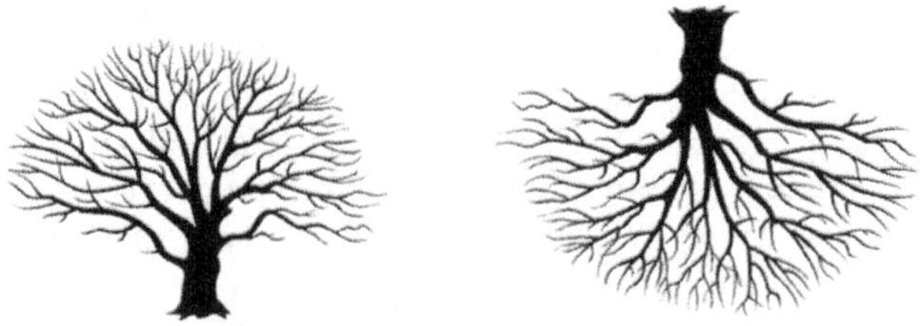

(a) (b)

Two views on how consciousness arises: (a) materialism where cognitive capacities arise out of the body; (b) reality is like an inverted tree where the root of the tree is Universal consciousness and the branches are various embodiments.

These are the six darśanas (complementary views) of Indian philosophy. The six are like the windows in the magic cube of our self and they may be viewed in three sets of paired views. First, atomic perspective on logic (nyāya) and matter (vaiśeṣika); second, analysis and synthesis of creation at the physical (sāṅkhya) and psychological levels (yoga); third, analysis of lived life (mīmāṃsā) and the cosmos (vedānta). Each of these views has its paradox that prepares for the intuitive leap to the next insight in the ladder of understanding. Partial understanding obtained from the darśanas may appear contradictory, but that is how one becomes ready for a deeper intuition.

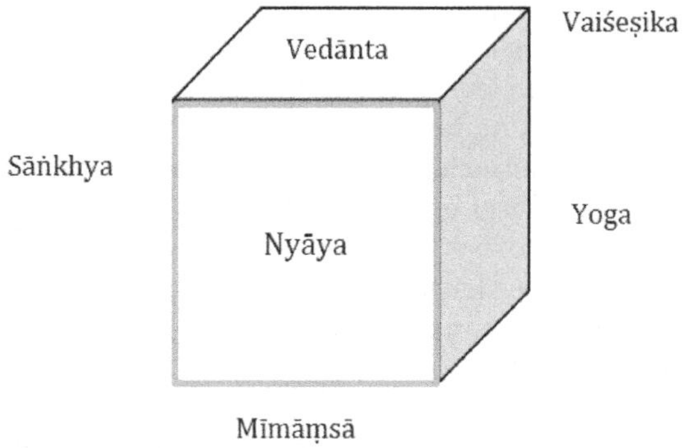

The magic cube: Mīmāṃsā is the floor, Sāṅkhya is the left side, Nyāya the front side, Yoga the right side, Vaiśeṣika the back, and Vedānta the ceiling

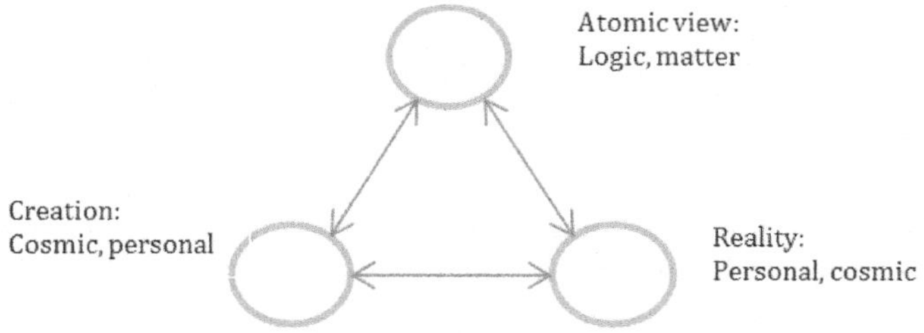

Magic cube as three sets of views

Atomic View

Although reality, whether experiential or physical, is continuous and connected, one can obtain insight by considering an atomic perspective on language and matter. The Nyāya analyzes perception as a relation between the senses (*indriyas*), their object (*artha*), the contact of the senses and the object (*sannikarṣa*), and the cognition produced by this contact (*jñāna*). The mind mediates between the self and the senses and when it is in contact with one sensory organ, it cannot be so with another. It is therefore atomic in dimension and due to this atomicity our experiences are essentially linear, although quick succession of impressions may give the appearance of simultaneity.

There are four kinds of perception: sense perception, mental perception, self-consciousness, and yogic perception. Self-consciousness is a perception of the self through its states of pleasure and pain. In yogic perception, one is able to comprehend the universe holistically.

The Vaiśeṣika defines seven categories of experience: substance, quality, action, universality, particularity, relation, and nonexistence. Substance is the most basic category, for it is in it that actions and qualities adhere. The Vaiśeṣika metaphysics is also atomic. Each atom possesses size and mass and is distinct from every other atom. Atoms can vibrate in groups and form dyads, triads and so on, until the combinations reach a diameter of one-millionth of an inch, at which state the substances can be identified as earth, or air, or fire, or water. The atom is point-like, for it could be sub-divided otherwise.

The Vaiśeṣika has categories not only for space-time-matter but also for attributes related to perception of matter. It starts with six nameable and knowable categories (*padārthas*). The categories are: *dravya* (substance), *guṇa* (quality), *karma* (motion), *sāmānya* (universal), *viśeṣa* (particularity), and *samavāya* (inherence). The first three of these have objective existence and the last three are a product of abstraction and intellectual discrimination.

The universals (sāmānya) are recurrent generic properties in substances, qualities, and motions. The particularities (viśeṣa) reside exclusively in the eternal, non-composite substances, that is, in the individual atoms, souls, and minds, and in the unitary substances ether, space, and time. Inherence (samavāya) is the relationship between entities that exist at the same time. It is the binding amongst categories that makes it possible for us to synthesize our experience.

The mind associates the non-substance categories with the substance. By doing so, it makes the observer central to the scheme. If there were no sentient beings in the universe then there would be no need for these categories.

There are nine classes of substances (*dravya*), some of which are non-atomic, some atomic, and others all-pervasive. The non-atomic ground is provided by the three substances of ether (*ākāśa*), space (*dik*), and time (*kāla*), which are unitary and indestructible; a further four, earth (*pṛthvī*), water (*āpas*), fire (*tejas*), and air (*vāyu*) are atomic composed of indivisible, and indestructible atoms (*aṇu*); self (*ātman*), which is the eighth, is omnipresent and eternal; and, lastly, the ninth, is the mind (*manas*), which is also eternal but of atomic dimensions, that is, infinitesimally small.

Of the substances, four (earth, water, fire, and air) are material (that is consisting of atoms) and capable of motion whereas five others (time, space, ether, ātman, and mind) are non-material and, therefore, no motion may be associated with them. In the scheme laid out in the system, ātman is listed before mind, suggesting that it is the medium through which mind's apprehensions are received. The atoms of earth, water, fire and air are different and this difference arises out of the different ways the fundamental atom of materiality combines with itself in different arrangements.

In the Vaiśeṣika system, observables arise through the effect of motion in a consistent manner. Although it has its own paradoxes, it offers a comprehensive view of the universe beginning with gross visible matter all the way up to the subtle invisible mind.

The atom is indivisible because it is a state to which no measurement can be attributed. What cannot be measured cannot be further divided and it cannot be spoken of as having parts. The motion the atom possesses is non-observable for the same reason and it may be viewed as an abstraction in a conventional sense. Space and time are the two lenses through which matter is observed and they form the matrix of universe.

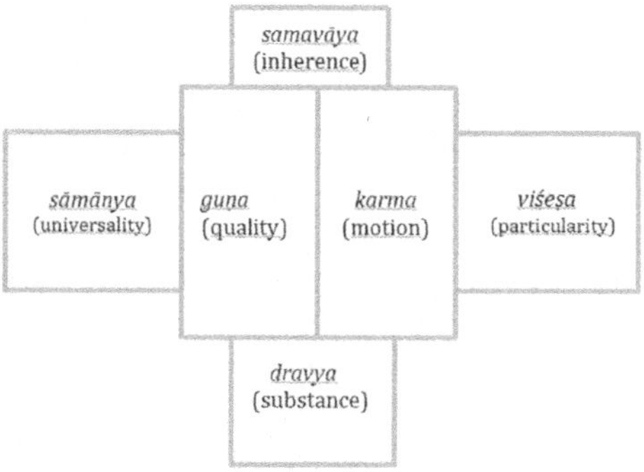

The six categories of Vaiśeṣika

The distinction between intrinsic (*karma*) and extrinsic (*kārya*) motions arises from the fact that unlike extrinsic motion, intrinsic motion is uniform in all directions. The intrinsic motion is like the motion of atoms within the matrix of matter.

When the universe ceases to be at the end of the cosmic cycle, matter is not annihilated; rather, it reaches a quiescent state where its atoms have no extrinsic motion and so become invisible, which is similar to the conception of the state of the giant atom at the beginning of the cycle of creation. The lack of motion represents a cessation of time, because time is a measure of change.

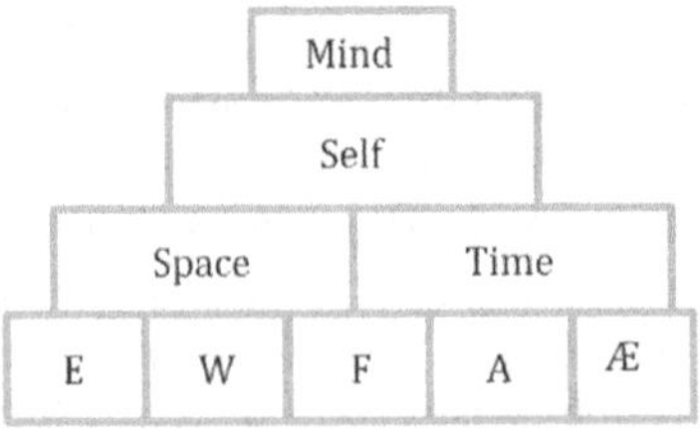

The nine *dravyas* (substances): E: earth; W: water; F: fire; A: air; Æ: ether

In the epistemology of the Vaiśeṣika system, one can obtain knowledge due to the agency of self. The atomic substances exist within the matrix of eternal substances. Materiality emerges out of the substratum of universal consciousness.

Creation and Evolution

The Sāṅkhya (sixth or seventh century BCE) is about the interplay between consciousness (*puruṣa*) and matter (*prakṛti*). Matter has attributes (*guṇas*) of *sattva* (transparence), *rajas* (activity), and *tamas* (inactivity). Prakṛti is inert when the three guṇas are in a state of equilibrium but when it comes into contact with puruṣa, the balance of the guṇas is destroyed, and this causes life to be created. The coming of the contact between the two categories implies that the two are not always present everywhere. In this coming together at the cosmic and the individual levels, the ratio between the guṇas changes. The first to emerge from prakṛti is *mahat*, the cosmic intelligence, and *buddhi*, the intelligence of the individual.

Out of *mahat*, the next lower category, ego (*ahaṅkāra*), is born; and out of the ego are born the individual mind (*manas*) and various organs of perception and action. When the bond between prakṛti and puruṣa is severed, the former regains its original equilibrium and again becomes inert.

The evolution of Sāṅkhya is both like modern evolution but also different in that it presupposes cosmic intelligence. Modern evolution implicitly uses intelligence when it speaks of optimization of function by Nature in its drive to select certain forms over others. Modern science takes consciousness to be an emergent local property whereas in sāṅkhya consciousness is an all-pervading category. In sāṅkhya, therefore, abstractions such as beauty are universals that are potential doorways to delve deeper in the nature of reality.

One can argue that the emergent forms are already present as potential in the system of laws and, therefore, the difference in the two points of view is only a semantic distinction. But an all-pervading consciousness has significant implications. Amongst other things it implies correlations across time and space that cannot be explained in the view of an emergent consciousness. Many individuals can speak of personal experiences that indicate such correlations. There is also evidence in the texts that relates to it. In particular, creative people often speak of their discoveries being made in a seemingly altered state of consciousness. Likewise, evidence of improbable scientific statements without context or theory that were proven correct centuries later will support the Vedic view of consciousness.

There are many passages in the Mahābhārata which describe the sāṅkhya system. It also insists that to the discerning, sāṅkhya and yoga are essentially one, as they complement each other. Sāṅkhya and yoga seem to be inextricably connected as far back as we can go. In the Bhagavad Gītā, there is much stress on *sāṅkhya-yoga* which is taken to be the same as the yoga of knowledge.

Since we comprehend the universe through our consciousness, in the Vedic systems the realization of the ultimate truth is through an understanding of the nature of consciousness.

Bhīṣma in the Mokṣadharma Book of the Mahābhārata says this of sāṅkhya and yoga together: "The followers of sāṅkhya praise the sāṅkhya system and the yogins praise the yoga system. Each calls his own system to be the better... The insights of yoga are addressed to the senses; those of sāṅkhya are based on texts (analysis). Both systems are approved by me. If practiced correctly, both would make it possible for a person to attain to the highest end. In both, purity as well as compassion towards all creatures is equally recommended."

The Bhagavad Gītā says in 5.5:

yat sāṅkhyaiḥ prāpyate sthānaṃ
tad yogair api gamyate
ekaṃ sāṅkhyaṃ ca yogaṃ ca
yaḥ paśyati sa paśyati

The place attained by sāṅkhya
is also reached by yoga
sāṅkhya and yoga are one.
He who sees this, truly sees.

Interpretation of language and reality

The interpretation of language is the concern of the mīmāṃsā. Mīmāṃsā thinkers argued that ascertaining the falsity of a proposition was as important as ascertaining its truth. If mīmāṃsā represents the analysis of traditional knowledge, the vedānta is knowledge at its deepest level.

According to the vedānta, there are two types of knowledge: empirical knowledge of the senses and transcendent knowledge. There are four states of consciousness: waking, dreaming, deep sleep and *turīya*. In *turīya*, one realizes that while the world of objects is real, it is not the ultimate reality. Behind the world of empirical reality is the ultimate reality of the Brahman, which is both immanent and transcendent and the cause of all phenomena. The individual self is simply an individuated aspect of Brahman. The world is created by Brahman and in the end becomes again a part of Brahman. The illusion of taking the physical world to be the only objective reality is *māyā*. Conscious mind is an epiphenomenon, because the individual self which is pure consciousness is not conscious.

The *mahāvākyas* or great sayings of the Upaniṣads summarize general characteristics of the self:

1. *prajñānam brahma,* Consciousness is Brahman. *(Aitareya Upaniṣad 3.3* of the Ṛgveda*)*. The basis of reality is World-Consciousness. Without consciousness there would not be reality since the universe would be dead.
2. *ayam ātmā brahma,* This self (ātman) is Brahman. *(Māṇḍūkya Upaniṣad 1.2* of the Atharvaveda*)*. There is only consciousness since otherwise there would be a multitude of universes.
3. *tat tvam asi,* Thou art that. *(Chāndogya Upaniṣad 6.8.7* of the Sāmaveda*)*. Brahman is also the embodied universe and therefore whatever is said of it is true.
4. *aham brahmāsmi,* I am Brahman. *(Bṛhadāraṇyaka Upaniṣad 1.4.10* of the Yajurveda*)*. The innermost being of the individual is the self.

There are other important mahāvākyas that take us to the heart of Vedic wisdom. Below are six statements that have become very popular in the general public:

1. *neti neti,* Not this, not this. It is the obverse side of *tat tvam asi,* implying that as a transcendent reality no words can completely define it.
2. *yat piṇḍe tad brahmāṇḍe* (as in the cell, so in the cosmos). This expresses the relationship between the microcosm and the macrocosm, or the inner and the outer skies.
3. *brahma satyam jagan mithyā* (Brahman is real, the world is unreal). The words *real* and *unreal* here refer to what is part of the unfolding reality, whereas the "world" is the construction of the mind and, therefore, arbitrary since different individuals construct it differently.
4. *ekam evadvitīyam brahma* (Brahman is one, without a second). There is no reality other than Brahman, since if there was another entity other than it then Brahman could not be the World-Self.
5. *sarvam khalvidam brahma* (All of this is Brahman). This is again because Reality must be equivalent to the World-Self.
6. *sacchidānanda brahma* (Brahman is reality, mind, and bliss). Brahman cannot just be materiality; it is also mind which constructs theories and the emotion of bliss that makes it worthwhile.

The Mahā Upaniṣad has a lucid analysis of the self by the sage Śuka that shows how logical analysis of self leads to paradoxes:

The self (*ātman*) is like an atom of ether (*ākāśa*) but more subtle. In this atom zillions of light particles are born and destroyed by its energy. Being consciousness, it is different from ether but having no physical form it is of ether. Its form cannot be described as it is not a thing, but it has power so it is substance.

Being of the essence of light, it is consciousness, but having no senses it is like inanimate rock. It causes the awakening of existence of the world in itself. The world being engendered within the self is not different from it. The differences in category that are seen in reality are not different from the self. Being connected to all, its movement is everywhere, but it does not move since there is nowhere to go. It does not exist as there is nowhere (substratum) to exist, yet exists because it is the basis of existence. Brahman is knowledge, bliss, and the basis of freedom and power. The wise say its understanding is beyond worldly conceptions. The dissolution and creation of the universe are due to the contraction and expansion of its powers.

V. Light and Time

The understanding of the atomic self is arrived at by inner light. The outer and inner lights have similar nature.

The atom's potentiality manifests in distinct attributes based on state of conjunction and motion. It is this potentiality that leads to diverse complex atoms with different attributes. These attributes may be viewed as being created by the matrix of space, time and number. Light has a special place in this view as it is both an elementary constituent of matter as well as the medium that shines the inner space of the mind. The atom of light cannot be described fully.

In the Kashmir school of Śaivism, both outer and inner realities (consciousness) are characterized by vibration (*spanda*) and it is this vibration that makes self-referral possible. The ultimate movement takes place not in space and time but inside consciousness. In this view *prakāśa*, the light of consciousness, and *vimarśa*, awareness of this light, are joined together.

The divisibility and flux of time is an apparent phenomenon, which is the shadow of the permanent and absolute time of Brahman. Phenomenal time is seen in cycles. The creation of the world is whimsical and is seen as a sport; on being accomplished the evolution of the world proceeds by natural law.

The Vedic view defines a world governed entirely by well-defined physical and psychological principles. These principles can be discovered by means of systematic observation. Human behavior is ordinarily determined by innate tendencies and the environment. The world normally appears material but if one believed in the interaction of mind and matter then it appears as dual.

At one level the Vedic world-view is quite in agreement with the scientific approach; at another level it extols the opposite approach of seeking the causes behind events. The Indian view of consciousness -- that it is a unity and the feeling of sentient beings as being separated from others is a misapprehension -- was endorsed by the physicist Erwin Schrödinger in his book *What is Life?* Indian tradition accepts that consciousness influences nature by the process of observation (*dṛṣṭi* in Sanskrit). This is very similar to the quantum mechanical view of the influence of observation on a physical process by the quantum Zeno effect.

But the difference between quantum theory and Indian ideas is that although one speaks of observations in quantum theory there is no place in its ontology for observers. Schrödinger was aware of this limitation of quantum theory and he argued that sense-categories like the tanmātras of the Sāṅkhya system of creation at the individual or the cosmic level were essential to understanding reality.

In traditional art Śiva (representing individual and universal consciousness) is shown as lifeless next to the vibrant Goddess (who represents Nature). Abstract representations of the cosmos show Śiva as a dot (of immateriality) within the (geometric) framework of the material world. Much of Indian mythology is an exposition of Indian epistemology in a coded language.

VI. The Saṃskāra Theory

How is a person driven to his actions? This is due to the workings of the *saṃskāras* that are latent impressions. The child is born with certain potential but what he achieves depends on his experiences that shape him when he is particularly impressionable. There are critical periods in childhood when the impressions are especially lasting. This is something like the critical period in a songbird's life when the songs learnt are then repeated for the rest of the life.

The saṃskāras are perhaps traced most deeply in the first couple of years of the child's life but they continue to be formed over the entire life. The saṃskāras create the lens through which we perceive the world. We cannot do without them and, therefore, it is essential to create good saṃskāras in the individual. But they become blinkers and, therefore, one must eventually transcend them. The yogi during the peak experience is free of the influence of the saṃskāras but when he comes to his ordinary state of consciousness, the saṃskāras, as habits of mind, take over. The yogi has the capacity to break the hold of saṃskāras learnt in childhood.

The saṃskāras work through activators that either inhibit or encourage certain behavior. Some activators are genetically determined, but others result from experience and actions. Meditation (*dhyāna*) and self-study (*svādhyāya*) help block existing latent-activators or establish new ones. Patañjali claims that this process is difficult and painful. Thus both nature and nurture play a role and there is the ability of the mind to transcend its limitations.

Not each mental impression leads to the formation of an activator. Rather, the activators respond to inherited archetypes and those that are the fundamental patterns underlying everyday life. There are many kinds of saṃskāras such as *vegas,* impulsive, *sthiti-sthāpaka,* elastic, and *bhāvanā,* reproducing imagination.

It is not the saṃskāras alone that define the individual. The individual has three bodies: physical (*sthūla*), subtle (*sūkṣma*), and causal (*kāraṇa*). If the physical body is defined by the genetic inheritance of the individual, the subtle body is the inner self, and the causal body is the deeper unmanifested self, that makes the inner life of the individual possible. A person can be physically alive – as in the case of a brain-dead individual -- and yet not have subtle and causal bodies. The subtle body of a male can be female not because the individual is lacking male organs but because of the influence of the causal body.

Network models of the brain are in agreement with the broad ideas of Patañjali. In such models short-term memory is coded by persistent electrical activity in the brain. The connections between neurons gets strengthened if they fire in a similar way and weakened if they fire differently. These models also suppose that interconnections are characterized by spurious states that must be suppressed. According to one proposal the purpose of dream sleep is to *unlearn* or suppress the spurious states. It is noteworthy that Patañjali explicitly mentions spurious states (1.8-1.11).

VII. Yoga of the Bhagavad Gītā

The Bhagavad Gītā presents the crisis of a man filled with doubt and grief. Kṛṣṇa tells Arjuna that attachment to oneself and to others is the source of suffering and he instructs him in purposeful and liberating action. Kṛṣṇa shows Arjuna a cosmic vision that frees Arjuna from his self-preoccupied identity. Finally, Kṛṣṇa instructs Arjuna in how to perform correct action.

Arjuna's crisis on the battlefield is about fighting a battle where his own relatives and loved-ones are arrayed on the opposite side. Kṛṣṇa begins by describing the Yoga of Knowledge explaining that although contact with the objects of senses produces pleasure and pain, these are not lasting. Only the ātman is birthless, eternal, perpetual, and primeval and it is not slain when the body is slain. The uncontrolled mind is one's enemy whereas the controlled mind is the friend who leads to liberation. Extolling sāṅkhya as yoga of knowledge, Kṛṣṇa defines yoga as indifference to success or failure, and skill in action.

Next he explains the Yoga of Action of the yogis, urging Arjuna to perform action without attachment to results. Normal action is merely guṇas acting on guṇas. Desire and anger, born of passion, conceal true knowledge. But one cannot run away from action and dilemmas of life. "Better one's own duty deficient than the duty of another well performed," he says.

In the Yoga of Renunciation of Action in Knowledge, Kṛṣṇa states that paradoxically one must see action in inaction, and inaction in action to be set free of compulsive desire. "Better than the sacrifice of material objects is the sacrifice of knowledge. All action is fully comprehended in knowledge. He who possesses faith attains knowledge and restraining his senses he attains supreme peace," he states.

In the Yoga of Renunciation, Kṛṣṇa says that yoga of action is superior to the renunciation of action. Insisting that sāṅkhya and yoga are essentially the same, he says the wise see in a cow, an elephant, a dog, a dog-eater and a wise Brahmin the same ātman. He whose self is unattached to external sensations and whose mind is united with Brahman through yoga finds imperishable happiness. The sage controls the senses, mind, and intelligence and he has overcome desire, fear, and anger. Kṛṣṇa now instructs how one is to sit in an āsana and learn to control the senses.

In the Yoga of Meditation, Kṛṣṇa instructs how one can advance one's practice by restraining the senses by the mind; he should fix his mind in the self. To learn to do yoga, one must perform action, but having mastered it, one is in a state of tranquility. "When one is attached neither to the objects of the senses nor to actions and one has renounced purpose, one has ascended to yoga," he says.

> For him who has conquered his self by the self,
> The self is a friend;
> But for whom the self is not conquered
> The self remains hostile, like an enemy. (BG 6.6)

Kṛṣṇa explains that the yogi's life should be that of moderation. The yogi finds the location of that infinite happiness which is grasped by the intelligence and transcends the senses, and, established there, does not deviate from the truth. (BG 6.21) Kṛṣṇa declares that the yogi's path is superior to that of ascetics, ritualists, and that of learned men.

In the Yoga of Knowledge and Discrimination, Kṛṣṇa distinguishes between the lower and the higher prakṛti: the lower prakṛti is matter whereas the higher prakṛti is the light of consciousness. He further declares that who sacrifice to the lesser gods in fact sacrifice to him.

In the Yoga of Imperishable Brahman, Kṛṣṇa speaks of the four categories of the *adhyātma* (the inherent nature of the individual), the *adhibhūta* (the perishable aspect of Prakṛti), the *adhidaivata* (the Supreme Divine Agent), and the *adhiyajña* (The Lord of the sacrifice) who is Kṛṣṇa himself. He asserts that meditating on him is *sulabha yoga*, or easy yoga. He also speaks of the nature of dissolution both at the individual and the cosmic levels.

In the Yoga of Royal Knowledge and of Royal Mastery, Kṛṣṇa speaks of himself as embodied Brahman stating, "Resting on my own material nature, I send forth again and again the multitude of beings. With me as overseer, material nature (prakṛti) produces all things animate and inanimate." He speaks of the deluded people in two classes: rākṣasa (acquisitive) and asura (materialists).

In the Yoga of Manifestation, Kṛṣṇa explains that the worship of all manifestation is his worship.

Next, Kṛṣṇa presents the Yoga of the Cosmic Form to Arjuna for which he first grants him divine eyes. Arjuna now sees all forms and time as a part of the vision which is like a thousand suns risen in the sky at the same time, one without beginning or end, with all the worlds pervaded by it. The cosmic form of Kṛṣṇa dispels Arjuna doubts.

In the chapter on the Yoga of Devotion, Kṛṣṇa assures Arjuna that being devoted to him, even in the absence of practice, will lead to perfection.

In the Yoga of Distinction between the Field-Knower and the Field, Kṛṣṇa explains the difference between puruṣa, the knower of the field, and prakṛti, the field of change. He explains that the knower of the field illumines the entire field. In the Yoga of the Distinction between the Three Guṇas, Kṛṣṇa explains the workings of the three guṇas of sattva, rajas, and tamas. In the next chapter, the Yoga of the Supreme Spirit, Kṛṣṇa explains how this world is like an inverted tree and the multiplicity one sees in it has the origin in the same seed, which is the supreme spirit. Next, in the Yoga of the Distinction between the Divine and the Demonic Destinies, Kṛṣṇa addresses the difference between godly (*daivī*) and demonic (*asuric*) forces. The demonic believe only in materiality, sense gratification, and wealth accumulation. They approach the world through desire, anger, and greed, which is the threefold gate of hell.

In the Yoga of the Distinction of the Three Kinds of Faith, Arjuna wishes to be instructed in what he should or should not do and the activity of the three guṇas. Kṛṣṇa elucidates these differences in terms of the yoga of freedom by renunciation wherein he again stresses the sacrifice of the fruits of action, the distinctions of the guṇas, and the cultivation of equanimity.

Finally, in the last chapter, the Yoga of Renunciation, Kṛṣṇa summarizes his instruction: "The Lord abides in the heart of all beings, causing them to move as a machine by the power of māyā." He now asks Arjuna to do what he thinks best. Arjuna announces: "Delusion is lost and wisdom gained by me through your grace. I stand with doubt dispelled and I shall do as you command."

VIII. Vasiṣṭha's Yoga

The Yoga Vāsiṣṭha, a great classic of yoga that was put together after the Yoga-Sutra, is a dialog between a despondent young Rāma and the sage

Vasiṣṭha. Rāma summarizes the sources of human suffering: impermanence, heartbreak, pain, illness, disease, and mortality. One cannot find happiness in things for they are like toys of which the child tires before long. But the desire for material objects is natural for a body-centric life. Rāma summarizes:

> In his youth, a man is a slave of sexual attraction. He perceives beauty and charm in the body. But soon the very flesh that contributed to the attractiveness is transformed into the shriveled ugliness of old age and later consumed by fire, worms, or vultures. Yet, while it lasts this sexual attraction consumes the heart and the wisdom of the man.
>
> When the child is dissatisfied with its childhood, youth takes over; when youth is plagued by dissatisfaction and frustration, old age overpowers it. Like the wind that tosses a dew-drop from the leaf, old age destroys the body. Like poison, senility pervades the body and breaks it down and makes it the laughing stock of other people.
>
> Even as the old man is unable to fulfill his physical desires, new questions torment him. He begins to ask "Who am I? What should I do?" when it is too late for him to change the course of his life. With senility further distressing symptoms appear.

Vasiṣṭha's teaching is to seek the higher planes of life in which one is attuned to the universal rhythms of life. In the universal frame, one is not different from others and, therefore, the cause of suffering vanishes. Vasiṣṭha concludes:

> What you have called the body does not exist in the eyes of the sage. Even the conception of the world as dream is not correct since there is no dream in the infinite consciousness. There is neither a body nor a dream in it, and neither a waking state, nor sleep. Between *this* and *that* is the body of consciousness: it is unity and diversity. Fullness expands in infinity; and then the infinite alone exists as the world. Wherever consciousness conceives of creation, materiality emerges. Indivisible consciousness exists everywhere, and all that is also this creation.
>
> Though this universe seems to have existed for a long time and though it seems to be a functional reality, still it is pure void and it is no more than an imaginary city. Though people have experienced its existence, it does not exist: even as one sees one's own death in a dream. The unreal appears to be real. The reality and the unreality of the world are two aspects of the Supreme Being.

Vasiṣṭha instructs that the mind, its motions, its logic, and its assumed cause and projected results, as well as the process of observing the mind and observing that process must be continually cultivated. He adds that latent tendencies (saṃskāras) are behind physical, verbal, and mental actions. There are two kinds of latent tendencies: pure and impure. The pure ones lead to liberation and the impure ones to further bondage and suffering. The eternal is not attained by rites and rituals, by pilgrimage or wealth; it is only attained by the conquest of the mind, by the cultivation of wisdom.

Vasiṣṭha explains that self-control, spirit of enquiry, contentment, and good company are the four doorways to the realm of freedom.

According to Vāsiṣṭha Yoga, the subject exists because of the object, and the object is but a reflection of the subject. Duality cannot be if there is not one, and there is no meaning to unity if one alone exists. When real knowledge is gained, what remains is not expressible in words. Of that it cannot be said that it is one or that it is many. It is neither seer nor seen, neither subject nor object, neither this nor that. Neither unity nor diversity can be truly established as the truth for every thesis gives rise to its antithesis.

IX. Tantra and Śrī Vidyā

There are different systems of esoteric practices within the Vaiṣṇava, Śaiva, and Śākta traditions and their texts are called saṃhitā, āgama, and tantra, but now the term tantra is increasing applied to all of them. These texts describe different types of practices for spiritual advancement. These practices include *mantras*, *yantras* (diagrams), gestures (*mudrās*), āsanas, and initiation.

One of these tantras is about the great Goddess Lalitā, who is also known as Tripurasundarī, Mahārājñī and Rājarājeśvarī. She is the presiding deity of the most esoteric yogic practices associated with the Śrī Cakra (also called Śrī Yantra) that are collectively called Śrī Vidyā.

The Gods bridge the duality in the field of imagination and experience: Conversely, the projection into processes of time and change is through the agency of the Goddess. Consciousness and Nature are opposite sides of the same coin.

Sages have argued that tantra, the yogic journey turned inwards, is the quickest way to reaching the top of the ladder and become free. If yoga is control of the mind, attention, harmony of body and spirit, and the way of freedom, how is one to find any of these when one is continuously distracted by desires? Where is freedom if one is weighed down by the burden of one's past with its guilt and regret?

Each one of us is capable of one-pointed concentration if our life depends on that moment. This is the concentration of the warrior on the chaotic battlefield. The warrior observes everything, even if only by the corner of his eye. Protected by the shield of his discipline, he is able to ward off the assaults on his being. Truth, compassion, energy, fearlessness, and fortitude are his shield; he is never without protection and, therefore, he cannot be vanquished. He lives fully in the moment.

One doesn't have to be on the battlefield to live like a warrior: the individual who lives the life with this attitude is the yogi. Since no one is born a warrior, how to prepare oneself to become one? Another way to ask this question is how to deal with the suffering that exists in life and the fear of death? Śrī Vidyā practice leads to fearlessness and it endows us with strength and unparalleled intuition. It leads to the heart of beauty, desire, and power, making it possible for us to separate our being from elemental impulses.

As our ordinary conception of who we are is determined by name and form (*nāmarūpa*), this journey requires challenging our most basic beliefs related to our personal and social selves. One needs to travel to the deepest layers of our being wherein spring our desires, some of which are primal and others that are shaped by culture and experience. Since name and form belong to the realm of time and change, this path is that of the Goddess. This path may be quick, but it is filled with danger since it involves deconstructing one's self and arriving at a new synthesis. Our inner world is like a jungle with its attendant beasts and many kinds of mortal dangers. Just as one should not enter a land with unknown topography, deserts, and rivers, without being armed and equipped, one should not try to enter one's inner landscape without being prepared. Such a journey needs guidance from someone who has been there before and it should not be undertaken by one who is not ready for this adventure. This way of the warrior is not for the faint of heart.

The sage Śvetāśvatara, who belonged to the late Vedic period, asks in his Upaniṣad whether time (*kāla*) or nature (*svabhāva*), or necessity (*niyati*) or chance (*yādṛcchā*), or *Puruṣa* is the primary cause of this reality. He answers in a riddle that goes:

> *tamekanemi trivṛtaṃ ṣoḍaśāntaṃ*
> *śatārdhāraṃ viṃśatipratyarābhiḥ*
> *aṣṭakaiḥ ṣaḍbhirviśvarūpaikapāśaṃ*
> *trimārgabhedaṃ dvinimittaikamoham. 1.4*
>
> Who (like a wheel) has one felly with three tires, sixteen ends,
> fifty spokes, twenty counter-spokes,
> six sets of eight, one universal rope,
> with three paths and illusion arising from two views. SU 1.4

This looks like the description of a *yantra*, but we don't have enough information on how to proceed to draw it. The text doesn't also explain what knowledge is symbolically expressed in this yantra. An interpretation of these numbers as different categories of Sāṅkhya was provided by Śaṅkara (788-820) although he did not specifically address its graphical design.

We argue that this describes the Śrī Cakra. This might appear surprising at first because the Śvetāśvatara Upaniṣad extols Rudra-Śiva and the Śrī Cakra is associated with the Goddess. But Śiva does reside at the innermost point (*bindu*) of the Cakra along with the Goddess. Furthermore, SU 4.9 proclaims: *māyāṃ tu prakṛti vidyānmāyinaṃ tu maheśvaram,* consider Nature to be magical (*māyā*) and the Great Lord (*Maheśvara*) to be the one who has cast the spell (*māyin*). The Goddess is another name by which Nature is known, therefore the mystery of the Lord in the launching of the Universe can only be known through the Goddess. The identification of the Śrī Cakra in SU goes against the scholarly view that the Śrī Cakra is a post-major-Upaniṣadic innovation.

The *bindu* or dot in the innermost triangle of the Śrī Cakra represents the potential of the non-dual Śiva-Śakti. When this potential separates into *prakāśa* (the *aham* or I-consciousness, Śiva) and *vimarśa* (the *idam* or this-consciousness, Śakti) it is embodied into *nāda, kalā* and *bindu*. *Nāda* is the primal, unexpressed sound (interpreted by human ear as *oṃkāra*) and *kalā* is the "*kāma kalā*," the desire to create, which the Vedas tell us is the desire "May I be many" (Chāndogya Up. 6.2.1.3). *Bindu*, as the potential universe ready to separate into various categories is Mahātripurasundarī. Śiva as *Prakāśa* (luminosity or consciousness) realizes himself as "I am" through her for she is the *Vimarśa Śakti* (Nature as the reflector).

Within the Yogic tradition, it is stressed that tantra is part of the Vedas. In the Devī Sūkta (Ṛgveda 10.125), the Goddess describes herself as supreme. In the Śrī Sūkta of the Ṛgvedic hymns (appendices), the goddess Śrī is associated with prosperity, wealth, and fortune, and she is spoken of as deriving joy from trumpeting elephants. The Śrī Sūkta, addressed to Jātavedas of Fire, was invoked at the fire ritual. In Kauṭilya's Arthaśāstra (14.117.1) there is reference to the goddess being invoked for the protection of a fort. In the Bṛhadāraṇyaka Upaniṣad 7.4 there is a reference to the goddess Vāc.

The Vedic triads, together with the dyadic male and female components, enlarge through expansion (*prapañca*) so the universe is a projection (*vimarśa*) of the Absolute's self-illumination (*prakāśa*).

The supreme deity in the form of Śakti (*parāśakti*), Śrī as the great goddess (*mahādevī*) is one of the aspects of Lalitā Tripurasundarī. She has three manifestations: *sthūla*, or descriptive as image; *sūkṣma*, or subtle as mantra; and *parā*, or transcendent as *yantra* or *cakra*. She is also called Rājarājeśvarī or just Śrīdevī. Those who see the three representations as interrelated are called the followers of the *kaula* tradition, as has been the case with the Kashmiris.

In the South, the *Tirumantiram* (*Śrīmantra* in Sanskrit) of the *siddha* Tirumular knows Śrīvidyā. In the *Lalitāsahasranāma*, Lalitā is described in terms similar to those of Durgā. Lalitā is worshiped as the srividyā mantra and as the Śri Yantra.

The Śrīvidyā mantra is known in three forms: *kādi* (starting with *ka*), *hādi* (starting with *ha*), and *sādi* associated with Śri Manmatha, Lopāmudrā, and Durvāsā respectively. The mantra is divided into three parts, which represent three sections (*kūṭa* or *khaṇḍa*) of the image of the Goddess: *vāgbhavakūṭa, kāmarājakūṭa,* and *śaktikūṭa*.

The 18th century scholar Bhāskarāya maintained that the Śrīvidyā mantra is meant in Ṛgveda 5.47.4 where it is said: *catvāra īṃ bibharti kṣemayantaḥ*, "that with four *īṃ*s confers benefit". The *kādi* mantra (*pañcadaśākṣarī*) has four long ī vowels. According to some, the 16-syllable mantra (*ṣoḍaśākṣarī*) is obtained by adding the seed-syllable (*bījākṣara*) *śrīṃ* to the 15-syllable mantra.

The Śri Vidyā mantra is viewed as 37 syllables, representing the 36 *tattvas* of reality of Śaivism and the 37th transcendent Parāśiva state. These are divided into 11 for the *vāgbhavakūṭa*, 15 for the *kāmarājakūṭa*, and 11 for the *śaktikūṭa*.

X. The Śrī Cakra and Lalitā Tripurasundarī

The three cities in the name of Lalitā Tripurasundarī are that of the body, the mind, and the spirit, or that of will (*icchā*), knowledge (*jñāna*) and action (*kriyā*). They may also be seen as the knower, the means of knowledge, and the object of knowledge; the three guṇas of *sattva, rajas* and *tamas*; *agni* (fire), *sūrya* (sun) and *candra* (moon); *sṛṣṭi* (creation), *sthiti* (preservation) and *laya* (dissolution); intellect, feelings, and sensation; subject (*mātā*), instrument (*māna*), and object (*meya*) of all things; waking (*jāgrat*), dreaming (*svapna*) and dreamless sleep (*suṣupti*) states; as *ātma* (individual self), *antarātma* (inner being) and *paramātma* (supreme self) and also as past, present and future.

Her five triangles represent the *pañca bhūtas* (five elements). She holds five flowery arrows, noose, goad and bow. The noose is attachment, the goad is revulsion, the bow is the mind and the flowery arrows are the five sense objects. Their union is harmony or *samarasa*.

Śaṅkara (788-820) spoke of the Śri Cakra in the *Saundaryalaharī* (SL). Its 4 *Śrikaṇṭha* (upward pointing) and 5 *Śivayuvatī* (downward pointing) triangles, which create its 43 triangles are described in SL11. If we see Śrī Cakra's structure as consisting of three basic triangles, then within each triangle are lower hierarchical levels of two other triangles, of alternating polarity. The 42 outer triangles are arranged in four circles around the middle triangle, with counts of 8, 10, 10, and 14 in the four arrays. The Śrī Cakra is also associated with the cakras of the yogi's body. According to SL 14:

> *Fifty-six for earth (mūlādhāra); for water fifty-two (maṇi-pūraka),*
> *sixty-two for fire (svādhiṣṭhāna); for air fifty-four (anāhata),*
> *seventy-two for ether (viśuddhi); for mind sixty-four (ājña cakra)*
> *are the rays; even beyond these are your twin feet.*

The six *cakras* are classified in *granthis* (knots) of two. The lowest two cakras correspond to 108 rays, the middle two to 116, and highest two to 136 rays. I have argued elsewhere that this provides an explanation for the layout of the great Śiva temple at Prambanan in Indonesia.

The Śrī Cakra embodies the tripartite division of the cosmos into earth, atmosphere, and the sun, which is mirrored in the individual by the body, the breath, and the inner lamp of consciousness; it also represents the three parts of the body: neck to head, neck to navel, and navel to the bottom of the trunk. It is within the wheel of time (*kālacakra*), and it is both the human body (microcosm) and the universe (macrocosm). Its middle 43 triangles are surrounded by a circle of 8 petals that, in turn, is surrounded by a 16-petalled circle. At the outermost are 3 lines, called the *bhūpura*. They are also categorized into 9 circuits or *āvaraṇas*, where the *bhūpura* is the outermost *āvaraṇa*. These 9 *āvaraṇas* have 108 presiding Devis. In the Śrī Cakra *pūjā* they are systematically worshipped one by one with their names and mantras. The nine circuits symbolically indicate the successive phases in the process of becoming.

The Śrī Cakra

The nine cakras are compared in the Tripura Upaniṣad to the nine yogas, namely the eight familiar ones of Patañjali and the additional one of *sahaja*.

Lalitā Tripurasundarī's three śaktis, which are shown in the three corners of the inner triangle, are Bhagamālinī, Vajreśī, and Kāmeśvarī, who are associated with Brahmā, Viṣṇu, and Rudra. The central *bindu* is where the Goddess is united with Śiva, the Universal Consciousness.

Cakra pūjā or Yantra pūjā is the worship of the deity. Devi, the cosmic female force, is the first step of creation. The counterpoint male principle has three emanations: Rudra from the left, Brahmā from the middle, and Viṣṇu from the right. At the center of the Śrī Yantra is *kāmakalā*, which has three *bindus*. One is red, one is white and one is mixed. The red bindu is Kurukullā, the female form; the white *bindu* is Vārāhi the male form; and the mixed *bindu* is the union of Śiva and Śakti.

Looking at the Śrī Cakra from outside in within the circular part of the Yantra, we thus have one felly with 3 tires, 16 ends of the petals in the outer circle, and a total of 50 (8 petals and 42 triangles outside of the central one) "spokes", with 20 triangles in the middle two circuits that may be termed "counter-spokes", a total of six circuits of petals and triangles have either 8 or more than 8 members, the universal rope is the *bhūpura*, the three paths are the paths ruled by the guṇas embodied by the three Goddesses in the innermost triangle.

The Śrī Cakra maps the inner sky as one goes from outside to inside; it is also located in the body in terms of the 6 *cakras*. The count of 50 of the Śrī Cakra is mapped to 50 petals of the *cakras* as one goes from the base (*mūlādhāra*) to the *ājña cakra*. The specific number of lotuses is 4, 6, 10, 12, 16, and 2. The *sahasrāra cakra*'s 1000 petals parallel the infinity associated with the innermost triangle of the Śrī Cakra.

Inside the square are three concentric circles, girdles (mekhalā). The space between the square and three girdles is the Trailokyamohana cakra, or the cakra that enchants the three worlds; at this stage the adept sees himself as his social self completely immersed in the magic of life.

The Śri Yantra represents the inner cosmos, which has the framework of infinity and recursion across scale and time and a mirroring of the outer and the inner, the ritual associated with it is the heart of yajña. The yantra's closed, concentric circuits (maṇḍalas) are the nine planes of consciousness. Each plane is a stage on the ascent toward the Inner Self.

The vowels and consonants of Sanskrit are inscribed in the vertices of the Śri Yantra and also within the body of the practitioner. In each of the nine circuits (āvaraṇas) specific deities are invoked. The deities are like veils concealing the deeper essence. After the sādhaka has invoked all the devatās in the prescribed manner, he obtains an insight in which all the deities of the plane are fused to become the presiding deity of the circuit.

Given the overlap between the numbers described in the Śvetāśvatara Upaniṣad and those of the Śrī Yantra, the case for the two Yantras being the same is compelling. The conception of the Goddess as the Supreme power out of which all the Gods emerged, encountered in the Durgā Saptaśatī, existed at the time of the Śvetāśvatara Upaniṣad for it is also proclaimed in the Devī Sūkta of the Ṛgveda (10.125). Furthermore, there is evidence of yantric structures in India that go back to about 2000

BC as well as representations of the Goddess killing the buffalo demon from the Harappan period, so we are speaking here of a very ancient tradition.

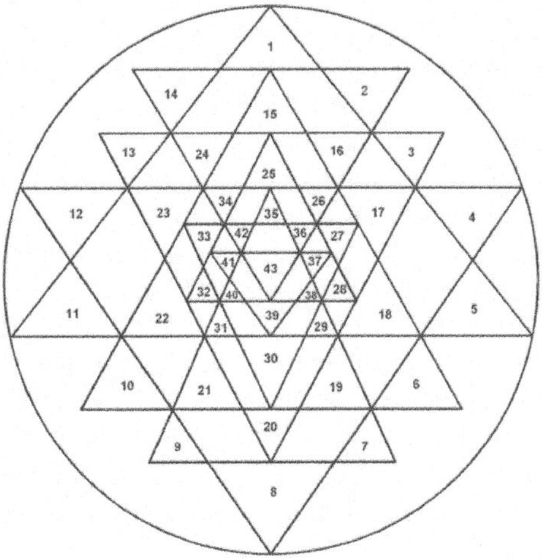

Forty-three triangles of the Śrī Cakra

The Śrī Cakra is an iconic representation of the deepest intuitions of the Vedas. It represents both the recursive structure of reality and also expresses the fact that Nature and Consciousness are interpenetrating.

XI. The Vijñānabhairava

The Vijñānabhairava is a text of Kashmir Śaivism that focuses on consciousness as freedom. Bhairava is a visualization of Śiva in which light of consciousness (*prakāśa*) and awareness (*vimarśa*) are fused together. The essential nature of Bhairava is *vijñāna* that leads to absolute freedom.
This text describes 112 dhāraṇās or types of yoga which are to be used based on the temperament of the practitioner. These types provide further nuance to Patañjali's eight limbs of yoga. These dhāraṇās include āsana, mudrā or gesture, prāṇāyāma, recitation of mantra, bhakti or devotion, jñāna, meditation, and bhāvanā (creative contemplation).
In contrast to the Yoga-Sūtra this text places greater emphasis on the nature of consciousness and its representation. This distinction carries over generally between the mainstream yoga and Kashmir Śaivism traditions.

XII. Cognitive Abilities

Naïve students of the Yoga-sūtra claim that yoga allows one to obtain miraculous powers (that go counter to scientific laws) based on the contents of the third part of the Yoga-sūtra that deals with *vibhūti* or *siddhi*. The sūtras speak of the yogi's ability to extend or strengthen the senses. Thus, *supernormal power of sight* is *extended vision*, as is made possible by television. By this we are not suggesting that Patañjali foresaw the invention of television, telephone and the like, but rather he intuited the possibility of mastery once the phenomena of vision, hearing, and so on were properly understood. There are other sutras that speak of the yogi being able to disappear or read the mind of another person. Such statements are not to be taken literally. That the non-literal interpretation is correct may be seen from the commentaries of Vyāsa, Vācaspati Miśra, and Hariharānanda Araṇya on the aphorism on the disappearance of the body. According to Vyāsa, the body disappears if the yogi ensures that the light regarding his body does not reach the viewer. Says Vācaspati: "When the power of being perceived is checked, then the yogi is no longer visible... The meaning is that the body of the yogi does not become the object of the other's knowledge." Says Araṇya:

> Magicians follow this system. They exert their will-power on the spectators who see only such things as the former want them to see.

Patañjali is really talking about sharpening the senses and he is also hinting at the complex relationship between the yogi and the layperson, in which the latter will often misconstrue what is being said. This makes clear individual aphorisms and when Book 3 is seen in entirety, this is the only interpretation possible.

It is true that the yogi controls processes within the body and the mind that are not accessible to the non-yogi. This control often lies outside what modern medicine considers possible. Swami Rama, a yogi who was famous in the late decades of the last century, whom I knew well, allowed doctors to perform experiments on him that confirmed he could control his autonomous nervous system in a manner that had been thought impossible. The yogi is also able to access the transcendent self within that gives him access to uncommon knowledge. The yogi's intuition and wisdom are extraordinary. In this sense, the yogi truly has miraculous powers.

The tradition speaks of eight different kinds of powers (siddhis) that are obtained by the yogi. According to one list, these are:

1. *ātma-siddhi.* Mastery over the self.
2. *vividhā-siddhi.* Mastery over the five tattvas.
3. *jñāna-siddhi.* Mastery of knowledge.
4. *tapaḥ-siddhi.* Indifference to the environment.
5. *kṣetra-siddhi.* Mastery over the environment.
6. *deva-siddhi.* Mastery over cognitive processes.

7. *śarīra-siddhi.* Mastery over the body.
8. *vikriyā-siddhi.* The capacity to transform to another.

In another enumeration, these are listed as the ability to make the body subtle, large, heavy, light, and so on. In yet other enumeration, mastery over different types of spiritual and worldly knowledge is listed.

=======

Most normal people who are non-yogis do not possess extraordinary abilities but this does not mean that such abilities do not exist. In fact one finds such abilities in the most artless people and in savants with severe disabilities. Although not all savants are autistic, the number of savants with autism is far greater than the number of savants without autism.

Savants are subnormal in most mental abilities with the exception of one or two areas in which they are extraordinarily gifted. They are known for feats of calendric calculations, photographic memory, musical virtuosity, or painting. A savant may have no sense of numerical abstraction and not add two small numbers but do other mathematical calculations almost instantaneously. Many savants are autistic; some others often have psychological disorders or mental illness.

One of most astonishingly musically talented savants was Thomas Wiggins. Born in 1849, he grew up a slave boy, blind and severely retarded on the Bethune plantation in Georgia. Tom would listen to the seven children in the Bethune family sing and play the piano. Once when allowed to the keyboard, Tom astounded the family that his small hands and fingers were able to reproduce the sequence of chords from his memory exactly as he had heard them played.

By age of six Tom started improvising on the piano and creating his own musical compositions. He claimed the wind, or the rain, or the birds had taught him the melody. A local music teacher told his master James Bethune that Tom's musical abilities were beyond comprehension and his best course of action was simply to let him hear fine playing. Bethune provided Tom with various music instructors. One of Tom's music teachers later reported that Tom could learn skills in a few hours that required other musicians years to perfect. In October 1857, James Bethune rented a concert hall in Columbus and for the first time Tom performed before a large audience. He was now hired out to a concert promoter who toured him extensively in the US, performing as often as four times a day. It has been estimated that based on the income he earned for his master, he was nineteenth century's most highly paid pianist.

Tom was different from other musical savants in that he possessed a degree of creativity and he could improvise on a song once he heard it. Tom knew literally every piece of music available in his day, including Beethoven, Mendelssohn, Bach, Chopin, Verdi, Rossini and Meyerbeer. It was estimated that he eventually developed a repertoire of several thousand songs.

Although Tom had a near perfect memory for any type of sound, he was so mentally deficient that he could only learn a few words with which to express himself. A newspaper account of him in 1862 says:

> The blind negro Tom has been performing here to a crowded house....He performs many pieces of his own conception-- one, his *Battle of Manassas*, may be called picturesque and sublime, a true conception of unaided, blind musical genius.... This poor blind boy is cursed with but little of human nature; he seems to be an unconscious agent acting as he is acted on, and his mind a vacant receptacle where Nature stores her jewels to recall them at her pleasure.

Mark Twain attended Blind Tom's concerts on three successive nights in 1869 about which he wrote thus:

> He lorded it over the emotions of his audience like an autocrat. He swept them like a storm, with his battle-pieces; he lulled them to rest again with melodies as tender as those we hear in dreams; he gladdened them with others that rippled through the charmed air as happily and cheerily as the riot the linnets make in California woods; and now and then he threw in queer imitations of the tuning of discordant harps and fiddles, and the groaning and wheezing of bag-pipes, that sent the rapt silence into tempests of laughter. And every time the audience applauded when a piece was finished, this happy innocent joined in and clapped his hands, too, and with vigorous emphasis...
>
> Some archangel, cast out of upper Heaven like another Satan, inhabits this coarse casket; and he comforts himself and makes his prison beautiful with thoughts and dreams and memories of another time... It is not Blind Tom that does these wonderful things and plays this wonderful music--it is the other party.

The account by his one-time music coach Anna Amalie Tutein that appeared in the Etude in 1918 is very revealing about the nature of the mind of an autistic savant. She shows how the sub-conscious mind of the savant appears to be autonomously performing at the extraordinary level. This is in consonance with the idea that capacities are autonomous and the mind is merely an instrument that keeps track of them. In a well-rounded person the various capacities are uniformly distributed and there exists substantial self-reflection which veils their true nature. The workings of the mind of the autistic savant reveal to us that many of our capacities have an unconscious basis.

When he was not engaged in playing or listening or eating, his favorite pastime was drawing circles with his hands upon the floor. Time and again he would draw circle after circle in a manner that was pathetic. During this he would stand upon one foot. He rarely said anything except what pertained to music.

Anna Amalie Tutein gives a very balanced portrayal of Blind Tom's compositions. She thought his compositions were "astonishingly interesting and often very beautiful." His playing was expressive and quite accurate. She adds:

> He never seemed to forget and could play such pieces as the *Sonata Pathetique* (which he studied in Germany) with surprising skill. His technical exercises were limited to a very few simple things that General Bethune's daughter had taught him. His playing was by no means a mirroring of the playing of others. He put in his own expression and exhibited much individuality. His octaves were very fine and clear and his great physical strength and elasticity made his playing forceful. It is a great mistake, however, to compare Tom with Franz Liszt. Liszt was, of course, an incomparable finer talent and intellect than Tom and his playing was accordingly finer. Tom, however, did play well and even better than many white contemporary pianists who made great pretentions and who took years to learn what Tom could learn in a few hours.
>
> How amazing this phenomenon was may be judged by the following fact that I could not myself believe possible if it had not been performed before my own eyes with a piece that I had taught him myself. When I had finished teaching him the solo part of the Beethoven *Third Concerto*, he amazed me by turning his back to the keyboard and playing the entire *Concerto* standing in that position. In other words, his right hand played the left hand part and his left hand played the right hand part...
>
> Now we come to that other mind-the diamond in the swine's mire. That it was something quite different from his conscious mind is shown by those strange indications of receptivity manifested by strange hissing sounds when his sub-conscious mind was working. This, according to reports, occurred from his earliest childhood. Stored up in that mind were many of the greatest treasures of music. It was also creative, in a limited and somewhat pathetic degree. That is, Blind Tom could compose. His compositions did not represent great masterpieces of harmony, form or counterpoint, but they indicated a desire to make new musical combinations. For the most part they were improvisations, and as far as my own quite extensive familiarity with musical literature goes, very original. He would play for hours at a time, occasionally one of the great masterpieces, and then going off into his interesting improvisations.

A computer-like sheer memorization does not explain the ability of savants such as Tom Wiggins, or that of others who can paint or sculpt extraordinarily well. Some mentally normal persons also have extraordinary abilities like that of autistic savants although that doesn't surprise us. This tells us that our understanding of the mind of the autistic savant tells us something about the normal mind.

Kim Peek, who died in 2009, was a more recent autistic savant who was the model for the character Raymond in the movie *Rainman*. Kim Peek had a photographic memory and he was able to read with his left eye and his right eye simultaneously, reading pages of text in seconds. He had memorized world history and he could accurately recall historical data.

Peek was born with damage to the cerebellum, and agenesis of the corpus callosum, a condition in which the bundle of nerves that connects the two hemispheres of the brain is missing. In Peek's case, secondary connectors such as the anterior commissure were also missing. It is possible that the neurons in the brain were wired differently due to the absence of a corpus callosum, which resulted in increased memory capacity. According to Peek's father, Kim was able to memorize things from before he had turned two. He read a book in about an hour, and remembered almost everything he had read, memorizing vast amounts of information in subjects ranging from history and literature, geography, and numbers to sports, music, and dates. According to a newspaper article, he could recall the content of at least 12,000 books.

=========

Of course, extraordinary cognitive capacity does not imply wisdom or spiritual advancement. That is why practitioners of yoga are advised that the miraculous powers are traps that make the true objective of yoga inaccessible.

A quantum basis to consciousness can potentially explain extraordinary abilities of certain people. But this cannot just be a quantum process arising out of the physiology of the brain, for it would then neither have the capacity to explain the behavior of savants nor the freedom of the individual. It will have to be a universal function which, when embodied in the neural structures of the brain, becomes subjective awareness. If this basis were to be scientifically validated, it could build a bridge between modern science and the intuitive understanding of the masters of yoga.

1. Concentration

प्रथमः समाधिपादः

अथ योगानुशासनम्॥१.१॥

atha yogānuśāsanam ॥1.1॥

1.1 Now commences the exposition of yoga.

Yoga in Sanskrit means "conjunction." Since there are many kinds of oppositions in the mind, there are a correspondingly large number of yogas. The yoga stressed in the Yoga-sūtra is that between the individual self (who operates based on conditioning, saṃskāras, habits) and the witness within. The witness is recognized as source of the voice with which one carries on a dialog in one's heart. By definition, the witness is detached; therefore yoga is to move the "location" of the individual self to that of the inner witness.

Yoga at the most basic level is to understand the relationship between the individual self and the witness. It is an exploration of the inner world and one component of that is the exploration of the body, since the two are interconnected.

Yoga is defined as *samatvam*, evenness of the mind, *karmasu kauśalam*, skill in action, and *duḥkha-saṃyoga-viyogam*, separation from union with pain, in the Bhagavad Gītā. It is defined as *sthirām-indriya-dhāraṇam*, control of the senses, in the Kaṭha Upaniṣad.

Yoga is training so that the witness (*upadraṣṭā*) is not just detached but in stages becomes the consenter (*anumantā*), the supporter (*bhartā*), the experiencer (*bhoktā*), and finally the master (*maheśvara*) as explained by Kṛṣṇa in BG 13.22.

According to the Vaiṣṇava text Ahirbudhnya Saṃhitā, the Yoga-Sūtra brings together in a systematic form material in the Hiraṇyagarbha text which is no longer available. Vācaspati says that Patañjali uses the word "*anuśāsana*" in the sense of "revised text."

योगश्चित्तवृत्तिनिरोधः॥१.२॥

yogaścittavṛttinirodhaḥ ॥1.2॥

1.2 Yoga is restraining the fluctuations of the mind.

The mind (*citta* here) is the instrument through which the individual self operates. *Citta* is the complex of memories that a person possesses and these memories are like eddies that disturb the surface of water. These eddies characterize the individual when he acts driven by his senses and his habits. Strictly speaking, the mind is the perceiving self and the bank of memories. But there is another self within each individual who is normally recognized as the *witness* with whom one is often in conversation. When the surface of water in the pool of the mind is still, it is representative of the witness.

The self and the witness are not located at any specific places in the brain. If they did, one could equate these places with the center of the mind which leads to the homunculus problem. The memories that the mind accesses are neither fixed entirely nor always accessible and yet there is a sense of continuity in the self.

The activity of the mind is caused by its three qualities: *sattva* (illumination and transparence), *rajas* (energy and activity), and *tamas* (veiling and inertia) and it is the interplay of the three that causes the same mind to indulge in different behaviors. Vyāsa reminds us that consciousness does not change and it does not go from object to object. Rather, objects are shown to it.

The fluctuations may be set forth by suggestion. Some patients who suffer harmful side effects do so only because they have been told to expect them. Similarly, people who believe they have a high risk of certain diseases are more likely to get them than people with the same risk factors who believe they have a low risk.

तदा द्रष्टुः स्वरूपेऽवस्थानम्॥१.३॥

tadā draṣṭuḥ svarūpe'vasthānam ॥1.3॥

1.3 Then the seer (that is, the self) abides in his own nature.

When the fluctuations are stilled, the self is one with the witness. This means that the self is not contingent on the memories sweeping across the mind. Its true nature is independent of memories.

When the states of mind are removed, the self does not become like a log of wood. Rather, it abides in its own nature as pure consciousness. It is like the sun, whose light shows the contours and texture of different objects, but which has no shape of its own.

वृत्तिसारूप्यम् इतरत्र॥१.४॥

vṛttisārūpyam itaratra ॥1.4॥

1.4 Otherwise he assumes the form of the fluctuations [of the mind].

If not abiding in itself, the self is defined by its momentary concerns. Because then the self is nothing but the contents of the mind.

Vyāsa says that consciousness (puruṣa) is not affected by the modifications of the mind in its ongoing activity. Knowledge is unity and yet knowledge is discrimination is how Ācārya Pañcaśikhā puts it.

Vācaspati says that the mind is not conjoined to the puruṣa; it is merely placed near it. The nearness of puruṣa is not in space or time on account of absence of juxtaposition. The puruṣa possesses the power of enjoying as subject, while the mind possesses the power of being enjoyed.

वृत्तयः पञ्चतय्यः क्लिष्टा अक्लिष्टाः ॥१.५॥

vṛttayaḥ pañcatayyaḥ kliṣṭā akliṣṭāḥ ॥1.5॥

1.5 The fluctuations are painful or not and they are of five kinds.

The specific memories have emotional content which makes some of them pleasant and others unpleasant.

Vācaspati reminds us that all beings are born with desire. The mental modifications of all living beings are therefore painful. Misery is the human condition as poets and writers have complained.

प्रमाणविपर्ययविकल्पनिद्रास्मृतयः ॥१.६॥

pramāṇaviparyayavikalpanidrāsmṛtayaḥ ॥1.6॥

1.6 These are: valid knowledge, misconception, conceptualization, sleep and memory.

The five states of the mind are valid knowledge (which is a judgment), misconception (which is a wrong judgment), conceptualization (abstraction), sleep, and memory (which in itself can never be perfect). Memory, as it is recalled, depends on the emotional state of the mind.

The *vṛttis* or fluctuations are the five-fold way in which the mind works. These five do not belong to the same class. Whereas the first two are right or wrong knowledge, the third is abstraction, the fourth is absence of reaction to ongoing processes, and the fifth is the store of earlier impressions. Memories as well as abstractions can also be wrong due to the inherent recursion in mind's processes. In reality, the vṛttis can also be a mixture of these five.

Placebos can improve health and fight disease. The converse of the placebo effect is the nocebo effect, in which dummy pills and negative expectations produce harmful effects. Voodoo death itself is an extreme form of the nocebo phenomenon.

प्रत्यक्षानुमानागमाः प्रमाणानि ॥१.७॥

pratyakṣānumānāgamāḥ pramāṇāni ||1.7||

1.7 Valid knowledge arises out of perception, inference and testimony.

If valid knowledge can only be obtained by the senses (or by their extensions), inference, and testimony, it can only be logical knowledge. This means that valid knowledge is a construction of reality which will fall short of representing its transcendent basis. Valid knowledge is, therefore, aparā or ordinary knowledge.

Perception is either a single state or a sequence of states that combine to form an aggregated state. Ordinary perception is an aggregated state and due to the limitations of the capacity of the senses as well as that of memory, it can only be an approximation of an event. Inference involves logical extrapolation on the available information.

When we speak of testimony, we are speaking of a competent man describing an object perceived or inferred by him. In other words, not all our knowledge can be based on our own direct apprehensions, but as social creatures part of this knowledge is derived from the testimony of others.

विपर्ययो मिथ्याज्ञानम् अतद्रूपप्रतिष्ठम्॥१.८॥

viparyayo mithyājñānam atadrūpapratiṣṭham ||1.8||

1.8 Misconception is false, illusory belief, not based on fact.

This implies that the mind has the capacity to create its own logic that need not correspond to that of reality.

As a result of saṃskāras the mind imposes its own structure on what it perceives. Parts of this structure are valid knowledge but other parts do not correspond to reality.

The structuring of reality by the mind is known to neuroscientists. Although extreme behavior of the mind is seen in patients with injuries, such behavior also underpins the workings of the normal mind. It can enter counterintuitive states such as alexia without agraphia or pure word blindness. Such a patient has the ability to write, but is unable to read even words that he just wrote. The ability to process visual input into language is lost in these patients. Prosopagnosia is a disorder of face perception where the ability to recognize faces is impaired, while the ability to recognize other objects may be relatively intact.

Prodigious savants have abilities that would be considered extraordinary even in a person without any limitations or special diagnosis of impairment. The most common trait of these prodigious savants is their seemingly limitless mnemonic skills, with many having eidetic or photographic memories.

शब्दज्ञानानुपाती वस्तुशून्यो विकल्पः॥१.९॥

śabdajñānānupātī vastuśūnyo vikalpaḥ ॥1.9॥

1.9 Conceptualization arises out of words and it does not need a perceptible object.

The conceptions of the mind or imaginations are built of words which, in themselves, are symbols that denote basic associations. The manner in which the words are further arranged has within it the power to create new conceptions.

According to Vyāsa, imagination is followed in sequence by verbal knowledge and expression and is devoid of objective basis. It is neither real nor unreal cognition but it is based on the power of verbal expression. As example, he mentions the statement: Puruṣa is of the nature of consciousness where we cannot say what is predicated on what since Puruṣa is consciousness itself.

अभावप्रत्ययालम्बना वृत्तिर्निद्रा॥१.१०॥

abhāvapratyayālambanā vṛttirnidrā ॥1.10॥

1.10 Sleep is the fluctuations of the mind with nothingness as substratum.

Sleep has influence on the succeeding waking state. "Good sleep" is what makes one feel bright and eager whereas "bad sleep" leaves one heavy and lethargic. If waking state is associated with the fluctuations of the *citta,* where do the fluctuations of sleep play out? In reality, there are different kinds of sleep states: dreaming, dreamless, as well that of *lucid dreaming.* Even in waking one goes through episodes of dream states, so that it is not really unique to sleep.

Vyāsa says that sleep is a state since its effect can be ascertained upon waking. This is seen in examples such as:

- I have slept well. My mind is clear.
- I slept badly; my mind is listless.
- I slept stupidly: my limbs are tired and mind is heavy.

The vṛttis caused by sleep thus need to be ascertained.

अनुभूतविषयासंप्रमोषः स्मृतिः॥१.११॥

anubhūtaviṣayāsaṃpramoṣaḥ smṛtiḥ ॥1.11॥

1.11 Memory is the recall of earlier experience of an object.

The recall of the earlier experience of the object is not quite exact and it is colored by the state of the mind and the amount of one-pointedness of the mind at the time of recall.

Vyāsa raises other interesting issues related to memory. First, memory is two-fold: when the phenomenon to be remembered has become the very nature of the mind as in dream, and when it has not so become as in waking. Second, does the mind remember the act of knowing or the object? Both of these play part leading to the formation of a habit. The habit manifests its own cause and generates a memory, having both the object and the act of knowledge as components. The act is manifested as a modification of intellect (buddhi), whereas the object is manifested as modification of memory.

अभ्यासवैराग्याभ्यां तन्निरोधः ॥१.१२॥

abhyāsavairāgyābhyāṃ tannirodhaḥ ॥1.12॥

1.12 By practice and detachment the fluctuations of the mind are restrained.

The fluctuations of the mind can be restrained by practice. Does the individual have the freedom to do the practice or is that a part of the conditioning of the individual?

The unfolding of the mind occurs both towards good and evil. That which flows to independence and freedom is called the stream of happiness and that which flows to indiscriminate ignorance or materiality is called the stream of sin.

This dichotomy of good or evil is stressed repeatedly in the Vedas as the way of the devas (gods) and the way of the asuras (demons).

तत्र स्थितौ यत्नोऽभ्यासः ॥१.१३॥

tatra sthitau yatno'bhyāsaḥ ॥1.13॥

1.13 Effort to acquire a stable state of the mind is practice.

Practice is the effort to secure steadiness. But behind the effort lies the desire for transformation. The desire springs from deep dissatisfaction with the present condition and by the fundamental property of the mind to fulfill itself.

स तु दीर्घकालनैरन्तर्यसत्कारासेवितो दृढभूमिः ॥१.१४॥

sa tu dīrghakālanairantaryasatkārāsevito dṛḍhabhūmiḥ ॥1.14॥

1.14 This practice is firmly grounded if it is cultivated properly for a long time.

The process of the firm grounding of practice requires patience. This means that the neural structure of the brain imposes its own constraints on how fast we can learn.

Also, the rate of our progress in our practice depends on our temperament and our natural abilities.

दृष्टानुश्रविकविषयवितृष्णस्य वशीकारसंज्ञा वैराग्यम्॥१.१५॥

dṛṣṭānuśravikaviṣayavitṛṣṇasya vaśīkārasaṃjṇā vairāgyam ||1.15||

1.15 Detachment is the awareness that one has no craving for earthly objects or miracles.

The awareness of detachment springs from letting the witness take control, which involves letting go. The letting go is accompanied by detachment from worldly possessions since one has a powerful awareness of being part of something much greater than oneself.

तत्परं पुरुषख्यातेर्गुणवैतृष्ण्यम्॥१.१६॥

tatparaṃ puruṣakhyāterguṇavaitṛṣṇyam ||1.16||

1.16 Awareness of the self and indifference to the attributes leads to supreme discernment.

The indifference is a consequence of the recognition that the self within oneself is the same as the self in every other being.

वितर्कविचारानन्दास्मितारूपानुगमात् संप्रज्ञातः॥१.१७॥

Vitarkavicārānandāsmitārupānugamāt saṃprajñātaḥ ||1.17||

1.17 Awareness arises out of deliberation, reflection, joy or egoism.

The awareness of oneness with the witnessing self is a consequence of much reflection which involves going back and forth between the two opposing banks of our existence, namely that of one's immediate self and the other of the larger self that includes the universe.

विरामप्रत्ययाभ्यासपूर्वः संस्कारशेषोऽन्यः॥१.१८॥

virāmapratyayābhyāsapūrvaḥ saṃskāraśeṣo'nyaḥ ||1.18||

1.18 There is another awareness that consists of latent impressions only, and it follows the practice of quieting the fluctuations of the mind.

A part of the awareness is that constructed by the saṃskāras. They are the window through which we see reality. There is an ongoing push and pull between what we do, our habits, and our conceptions.

This has been validated by neuroscience. We now know that the very organization of the brain is affected by its experience. The brain is a self-organizing system.

भवप्रत्ययो विदेहप्रकृतिलयानाम्॥१.१९॥

bhavapratyayo videhaprakṛtilayānām ॥1.19॥

1.19 Concentration allows one to merge, bodiless, in the essence of the nature of the subject.

The mind has the capacity to be free in many different ways so that if we focus we can merge, bodiless, in the essence of the object of our concentration. This merging happens both in imagined or recounted experience or action of oneself or the experience or action as some other individual.

श्रद्धावीर्यस्मृतिसमाधिप्रज्ञापूर्वक इतरेषाम्॥१.२०॥

śraddhāvīryasmṛtisamādhiprajñāpūrvaka itareṣām ॥1.20॥

1.20 Belief, energy, mindfulness, concentration and insight lead to latent impressions.

The saṃskāras are not established only during childhood although that is when experiences have the most powerful effect on the growing brain and the developing mind.

Our actions keep on modifying our mind and brain. Thoughts create latent impressions. Our thoughts modify our brain.

तीव्रसंवेगानाम् आसन्नः॥१.२१॥

tīvrasaṃvegānām āsannaḥ ॥1.21॥

1.21 For the very intense, self-realization is speedy.

The processes of the mind can be speeded up by very intense practice. This reinforces the previous sūtra.

मृदुमध्याधिमात्रत्वात् ततोऽपि विशेषः॥१.२२॥

mṛdumadhyādhimātratvāt tato'pi viśeṣaḥ ॥1.22॥

1.22 The degree of intensity decides the nearness of the goal.

The degree of intensity is correlated with how soon one reaches the goal.

ईश्वरप्रणिधानाद् वा॥१.२३॥

īśvarapraṇidhānād vā ॥1.23॥

1.23 Concentration is attained by devotion to the self.

The realization that the enjoying self (consciousness, Īśvara) is present everywhere helps one attain concentration. But who is the enjoying self? For the simple-minded, the enjoyer is the autobiographical self. For those, who think they are nothing but their bodies, the pursuit of sensory pleasures can be accompanied by great concentration.

For the more discerning, the enjoyer comes wrapped in many covers: at the deepest level the enjoying self is without attributes. But in more embodied levels, one can see the enjoying self to have different attributes such as law, compassion, and intuition. In the embodied levels, the enjoying self is one's chosen deity.

क्लेशकर्मविपाकाशयैरपरामृष्टः पुरुषविशेष ईश्वरः॥१.२४॥

kleśakarmavipākāśayairaparāmṛṣṭaḥ puruṣaviśeṣa īśvaraḥ ॥1.24॥

1.24 The self is untouched by troubles, action, success, and memories.

Īśvara or the conscious self is untouched by emotions. He is pure witness who transcends time. It is this transcendence of time that makes him have no emotion.

तत्र निरतिशयं सर्वज्ञबीजम्॥१.२५॥

tatra niratiśayaṃ sarvajñabījam ॥1.25॥

1.25 In the self resides the seed of all knowledge.

In Īśvara reside the seed of all knowledge. In other words, by asking the question as to who the observer is, one can obtain insights and attain knowledge. It is also because Īśvara is beyond time and our ordinary knowledge may be seen to address the mystery of time.

स एष पूर्वेषामपि गुरुः कालेनानवच्छेदात्॥१.२६॥

sa eṣa pūrveṣāmapi guruḥ kālenānavacchedāt ॥1.26॥

1.26 The self led to the knowledge of the earlier masters also.

The same consciousness leads to the knowledge of the earlier teachers and gurus. Consciousness, therefore, is a category that transcends time.

तस्य वाचकः प्रणवः ॥१.२७॥

tasya vācakaḥ praṇavaḥ ॥1.27॥

1.27 Its symbol is the praṇava (the syllable om).

Its symbol in Sanskrit is Om. This syllable is taken as a measure of the embodied self. The Upaniṣads say that Om symbolizes the universe in that it has three syllables a, u, m just as the outer universe has three parts: earth, atmosphere, and the sun, and the inner universe also has three parts: body, breath, and the light of consciousness.

तज्जपस्तदर्थभावनम्॥१.२८॥

tajjapastadarthabhāvanam ॥1.28॥

1.28 The recitation of the syllable leads to the intuition of its meaning.

Recitation calms the mind, stills the fluctuations and thereby makes it easier for the mind to find balance and harmony. The three syllables resonate in the body.

ततः प्रत्यक्चेतनाधिगमोऽप्यन्तरायाभावश्च॥१.२९॥

tataḥ pratyakcetanādhigamo'pyantarāyābhavaśca ॥1.29॥

1.29 Then follows the attainment of inward-mindedness and a disappearance of obstacles.

The obstacles are external to the mind and, therefore, inward-mindedness helps in the development of one's intuition.

व्याधिस्त्यानसंशयप्रमादालस्याविरतिभ्रान्तिदर्शनालब्धभूमिकत्वानवस्थितत्वानि
चित्तविक्षेपास्तेऽन्तरायाः॥१.३०॥

vyādhistyānasaṃśayapramādālasyāviratibhrāntidarśanālabdha
bhūmikatvānavasthitatvāni cittavikṣepāste'ntarāyāḥ ॥1.30॥

1.30 The obstacles for the mind are: sickness, languor, doubt, heedlessness, sloth, dissipation, false vision and instability.

Mind and body are interconnected. If the mind is not in balance there are manifestations of this in various bodily ailments. The obstacles make it harder for one to imagine that one can be more than one's body.

दुःखदौर्मनस्याङ्गमेजयत्वश्वासप्रश्वासा विक्षेपसहभुवः॥१.३१॥

duḥkhadaurmanasyāṅgamejayatvaśvāsapraśvāsā vikṣepasahabhuvaḥ ॥1.31॥

1.31 The obstacles are accompanied by pain, depression, unsteadiness of body and breath.

The body's lack of balance leads to physical and mental pain.

तत्प्रतिषेधार्थम् एकतत्त्वाभ्यासः॥१.३२॥

tatpratiṣedhārtham ekatattvābhyāsaḥ ॥1.32॥

1.32 To check the obstacles one should concentrate on a single element.

If the body and mind are vast currents with interacting eddies, the conscious mind can only be at one place at a time. It becomes essential, therefore, to begin to control the mind and the body by starting with one single element in the multitude of processes that are going on. This concentration of a single element is like purifying the nerves that focus on that process.

मैत्रीकरुणामुदितोपेक्षणां सुखदुःखपुण्यापुण्यविषयाणां
भावनातश्चित्तप्रसादनम्॥१.३३॥

maitrī karuṇā muditopekṣaṇāṃ sukhaduḥkhapuṇyāpuṇyaviṣayāṇāṃ
bhāvanātaścittaprasādanam ॥1.33॥

1.33 The projection of friendliness, compassion, joy and equanimity for events whether they are happy or sad, praiseworthy or vile brings about a quieting of the mind.

Just like concentrating on a single element is helpful, so is projecting an attitude of compassion, friendliness, and joy.

प्रच्छर्दनविधारणाभ्यां वा प्राणस्य॥१.३४॥

pracchardanavidhāraṇābhyāṃ vā prāṇasya ॥1.34॥

1.34 The stability of the mind is aided by controlled breathing.

Controlled breathing puts us in touch with our body. One of the biggest problems of our times is the manner in which we are alienated from Nature and from our own selves. Controlled breathing addresses this problem by making the person more aware of the body. Controlled breathing also helps one measure out one's body.

विषयवती वा प्रवृत्तिरुत्पन्ना मनसः स्थितिनिबन्धिनी॥१.३५॥

viṣayavatī vā pravṛttirutpannā manasaḥ sthitinibandhinī ॥1.35॥

1.35 Object-centered activities hold the mind in steadfastness.

Object-centered activities move the person beyond selfish personal concerns and make him get closer to the universal. Why we like great stories is because they take us away from our concerns of the moment and make us part of a much larger presence.

विशोका वा ज्योतिष्मती॥१.३६॥

viśokā vā jyotiṣmatī ॥1.36॥

1.36 As activities that are painless and illuminating.

Painful activities are those in which we pity ourselves. Self-pity is like a prison that separates us from our true self. Contrariwise, painless lucidity steadies the mind.

वीतरागविषयं वा चित्तम्॥१.३७॥

vītarāgaviṣayam vā cittam ॥1.37॥

1.37 As reflection without passion.

Reflection with passion does not clarify. Without passion, the state of pure observation leads to steadiness.

स्वप्ननिद्राज्ञानालम्बनं वा॥१.३८॥

svapnanidrājñānālambanam vā ॥1.38॥

1.38 As reflection on the nature of dreams and sleep.

Reflecting on dreams and sleep is the first step in self-study.

यथाभिमतध्यानाद् वा॥१.३९॥

Yathābhimatadhyānād vā ॥1.39॥

1.39 As meditation on any other subject.

Or one may meditate on any subject one likes since the process of meditation and reflection is what causes change by separating oneself from conditioned response.

परमाणु परममहत्त्वान्तोऽस्य वशीकारः॥१.४०॥

paramāṇu paramamahattvānto'sya vaśīkāraḥ ॥1.40॥

1.40 Then mastery ranges from the smallest atom to the greatest object.

Once one has learnt to focus on single elements, one can then successively consider other elements as well as their aggregations.

क्षीणवृत्तेरभिजातस्येव मणेर्ग्रहीतृग्रहणग्राह्येषु तत्स्थतदञ्जनतासमापत्तिः॥१.४१॥

kṣīṇavṛtterabhijātasyeva maṇergrahītṛgrahaṇagrāhyeṣu tatsthatadañjanatā samāpattiḥ ॥1.41॥

1.41 When the fluctuations of the mind have dwindled away, the mind takes on the features of the object of meditation – whether it be the cognizer, the instrument of cognition or the object cognized – like a transparent jewel. This identification is called engrossment.

With meditation the mind falls away and it can become one with either the meditating self, the instrument of meditation, or its object.

तत्र शब्दार्थज्ञानविकल्पैः संकीर्णा सवितर्का समापत्तिः॥१.४२॥

tatra śabdārthajñānavikalpaiḥ saṃkīrṇā savitarkā samāpattiḥ ॥1.42॥

1.42 Engrossment in which there is coincidence of the word, its meaning and its knowledge is called cognitive engrossment.

Such meditation has an aspect related to meaning of words. It makes it possible to see deeper connections between words and elements of experience and consciousness.

स्मृतिपरिशुद्धौ स्वरूपशून्येवार्थमात्रनिर्भासा निर्वितर्का॥१.४३॥

smṛtipariśuddhau svarūpaśūnyevārthamātranirbhāsā nirvitarkā ॥1.43॥

1.43 On the purification of memory, the mind appears to be devoid of self-reflection and only the contemplated object remains illumined in a super-cognitive state.

Counterintuitively, one realizes that the mind which one normally identifies with one's inner self is an obstacle in our cognitions. One needs to destroy the mind to be oneself! When the mind is destroyed then one can contemplate objects in the most direct manner. One can also experience events with the greatest directness.

एतयैव सविचारा निर्विचारा च सूक्ष्मविषया व्याख्याता॥१.४४॥

etayaiva savicārā nirvicārā ca sūkṣmaviṣayā vyākhyātā ॥1.44॥

1.44 Similarly there are reflexive and super-reflexive engrossments that are propped up by subtle objects.

The direct experience of objects is a process that has its own subtle body as the ground.

सूक्ष्मविषयत्वं चालिङ्गपर्यवसानम्॥१.४५॥

sūkṣmaviṣayatvam cāliṇgaparyavasānam ॥1.45॥

1.45 Subtle objects terminate in the indifferentiate.

Slowly one finds the measure of the subtle body and sees that it terminates with the universal.

ता एव सबीजः समाधिः॥१.४६॥

tā eva sabījaḥ samādhiḥ ॥1.46॥

1.46 The engrossments belong to the class with seed.

These take us to engrossments that have a seed as the basis.

निर्विचारवैशारद्येऽध्यात्मप्रसादः॥१.४७॥

Nirvicāravaiśāradye'dhyātmaprasādaḥ ॥1.47॥

1.47 On gaining proficiency in the super-reflexive engrossment, purity in the inner instrument of cognition is developed.

ऋतंभरा तत्र प्रज्ञा॥१.४८॥

ṛtaṃbharā tatra prajñā ॥1.48॥

1.48 The intuition that arises is filled with truth.

This is deep intuition that is not connected to specific objective knowledge. It is a new way of knowing. It is the way of knowledge.

श्रुतानुमानप्रज्ञाभ्याम् अन्यविषया विशेषार्थत्वात्॥१.४९॥

Śrutānumānaprajñābhyām anyaviṣayā viśeṣārthatvāt ॥1.49॥

1.49 This intuition is different from that derived from testimony or inference, because they relate to particulars of objects.

तज्जः संस्कारोऽन्यसंस्कारप्रतिबन्धी॥१.५०॥

tajjaḥ saṃskāro'nyasaṃskārapratibandhī ॥1.50॥

1.50 The latent impressions born of this intuition obstruct other types of latent impressions.

The way to deeper intuition is to overcome saṃskāras.

तस्यापि निरोधे सर्वनिरोधान् निर्बीजः समाधिः॥१.५१॥

tasyāpi nirodhe sarvanirodhān nirbījaḥ samādhiḥ ॥1.51॥

1.51 When these saṃskāras are also restricted one gains seedless concentration.

We have seen how deep meditation takes us from a state of embodied concentration (which retains the modes of thought that we learnt from our saṃskāras) to seedless concentration (which is beyond words).

इति पतञ्जलिविरचिते योगसूत्रे प्रथमः समाधिपादः।

Here ends the first part of Patañjali's Yoga-sūtra on the concentration.

2. Means of Attainment

द्वितीयः साधनपादः

तपःस्वाध्यायेश्वरप्रणिधानानि क्रियायोगः ॥२.१॥

tapaḥ svādhyāyeśvarapraṇidhānāni kriyāyogaḥ ॥2.1॥

2.1 Discipline and devotion to self constitute the yoga of action.

Thoughtful life is yoga. Each person is on a self-made path of yoga but most lose their way for they lack proper guidance. The inner world is a dense and deep forest and it is helpful to have a guide who can point to different stations along the way that mark our progress. Without the guide or the grace that takes one in a million across the forest without a guide, the forest is like a labyrinth, a maze.

Even those who only recognize worldly success and sensate pleasures are on yogic path. The craving for a deeper physical or emotional experience is the craving for knowledge that each being possesses. The good yogic path is the one that has the capacity to take us across the deep and dense forest of our inner world.

समाधिभावनार्थः क्लेशतनूकरणार्थश्च॥२.२॥

samādhibhāvanārthaḥ kleśatanūkaraṇārthaśca ॥2.2॥

2.2 This is to bring about concentration and for the attenuation of hindrances.

The reason behind yoga of action is the need for discipline and for success.

अविद्यास्मितारागद्वेषाभिनिवेशाः क्लेशाः ॥२.३॥

avidyāsmitārāgadveṣābhiniveśaḥ kleśāḥ ॥2.3॥

2.3 Ignorance (avidyā), egoism, attachment, aversion, and fear of death are the hindrances.

Avidyā is the belief in radical materialism. It ignores the spiritual side of existence. Egoism is the false premise that one's success is entirely due to oneself, when it is clear that luck and circumstance play much role in that.

अविद्या क्षेत्रम् उत्तरेषां प्रसुप्ततनुविच्छिन्नोदाराणाम्॥२.४॥

avidyā kṣetram uttareṣām prasuptatanuvicchinnodārāṇām ||2.4||

2.4 Ignorance is the breeding ground for others whether they be dormant, attenuated, interrupted, or active.

Avidyā is the source of many other hindrances in our search for our true self. Sarvasāra Upaniṣad defines avidyā as all things that emphasize egoism whereas vidyā is what leads to the absence of egoism or what presents the universal perspective.

अनित्याशुचिदुःखानात्मसु नित्यशुचिसुखात्मख्यातिरविद्या॥२.५॥

anityāśuciduḥkhānātmasu nityaśucisukhātmakhyātiravidyā ||2.5||

2.5 Ignorance is seeing of eternal, pure, joyful, and the self in that which is ephemeral, impure, sorrowful, and the non-self.

दृग्दर्शनशक्त्योरेकात्मतेवास्मिता॥२.६॥

dṛgdarśanaśaktyorekātmatevāsmitā ||2.6||

2.6 Egoism is the identification, as it were, of the mechanics of seeing with the power by which one sees.

Egoism is to see the body as the source of knowledge. This view is at variance with the principle that we are only reacting to the processes around us in which case the body is not the source of knowledge at all.

सुखानुशयी रागः॥२.७॥

sukhānuśayī rāgaḥ ||2.7||

2.7 Attachment is that which rests on remembrance of pleasure.

This is the basis of associational memory which gets mapped at various levels down to that of neurons.

दुःखानुशयी द्वेषः॥२.८॥

duḥkhānuśayī dveṣaḥ ||2.8||

2.8 Aversion is that which rests on sorrowful experience.

This aversion is also seen at various levels in the brain down to the level of neurons. The brain itself is organized based on this principle. Linkages between the neurons that are engaged in similar activity are strengthened and the linkages between neurons that are engaged in dissimilar activity are weakened.

स्वरसवाही विदुषोऽपि तथारूढो भिनिवेशः॥२.९॥

svarasvāhī viduṣo'pi tathārūḍhobhiniveśaḥ ॥2.9॥

2.9 The will to live, flowing along by its own momentum, is rooted even in the wise.

The other principle that is basic to all life is the "will to live", not only in those who are driven primarily by instinct but also in the wise.

ते प्रतिप्रसवहेयाः सूक्ष्माः॥२.१०॥

te pratiprasavaheyāḥ sūkṣmāḥ ॥2.10॥

2.10 These hindrances, when they have become subtle, are overcome when they have run their course.

The hindrances are a consequence of the nature of the body and the saṃskāras associated with one's experience. These hindrances constitute the framework of the individual's mind. But when practice and knowledge make it possible for the yogi to dispose of the mind in relating to reality, the hindrances no longer exist.

ध्यानहेयास्तद्वृत्तयः॥२.११॥

dhyānaheyāstadvṛttayaḥ ॥2.11॥

2.11 The fluctuations of these are to be overcome by contemplation.

The hindrances in some form may yet afflict the yogi in actions as he reacts by instinct. Meditation or contemplation overcomes these residual fluctuations.

क्लेशमूलः कर्माशयो दृष्टादृष्टजन्मवेदनीयः॥२.१२॥

kleśamūlaḥ karmāśayo dṛṣṭādṛṣṭajanmavedanīyaḥ ॥2.12॥

2.12 The hindrances are the root of the action deposit and it may be seen in the present or in future.

The hindrances constitute a lens which shapes the understanding of the past as well the vision of the future. This lens is like the root out of which the tree of experience emerges.

सति मूले तद्विपाको जात्यायुर्भोगाः॥२.१३॥

sati mūle tadvipāko jātyāyurbhogāḥ ॥2.13॥

2.13 So long as the root exists there will be fruition from it: birth, life and enjoyment.

The complex emerging from this root is associated with birth, a life history and enjoyment.

ते ह्लादपरितापफलाः पुण्यापुण्यहेतुत्वात्॥२.१४॥

te hlādaparitāpaphalāḥ puṇyāpuṇyahetutvāt ॥2.14॥

2.14 These fruitions are joyous or distressful by reason of virtue or vice.

Virtue and vice may be defined in terms of what they do to the fruits of life-action. Virtue leads to joy and liberation whereas vice leads to bondage and pain.

परिणामतापसंस्कारदुःखैर्गुणवृत्तिविरोधाच् च दुःखम् एव सर्वं विवेकिनः॥२.१५॥

pariṇāmatāpasaṃskāraduḥkhairguṇavṛttivirodhāc ca duḥkham eva sarvaṃ vivekinaḥ ॥2.15॥

2.15 Due to the distress in the transformation of the saṃskāras and the sorrow in the conflict of the changing attributes to the discerner, all is but pain.

In reality life is painful to the discriminating individual as change necessitates conflict with the saṃskāras and one perceives that one is not what one is holding on to.

हेयं दुःखम् अनागतम्॥२.१६॥

heyaṃ duḥkham anāgatam ॥2.16॥

2.16 That which is to be avoided is pain yet-to-come.

Although one can do nothing about the pain experienced in the past, the pain to come in the future - if one did nothing with one's life - can be avoided.

द्रष्टृदृश्ययोः संयोगो हेयहेतुः॥२.१७॥

draṣṭṛdṛśyayoḥ saṃyogo heyahetuḥ ॥2.17॥

2.17 The conflation of the seer with the seen is the cause of that which is to be avoided.

The pain that one wishes to avoid is a consequence of the conflation of the seer with the seen. The seen is the material world around us, but the seer is the puruṣa who transcends all and is the witness within oneself. When the material is conflated with the spirit, life can only be seen as limiting and full of suffering as it is associated with loss and painful change and illness and death.

प्रकाशक्रियास्थितिशीलं भूतेन्द्रियात्मकं भोगापवर्गार्थं दृश्यम्॥२.१८॥

prakāśakriyāsthitiśīlaṃ bhūtendriyātmakaṃ bhogāpavargārthaṃ dṛśyam ॥2.18॥

2.18 The seen has the characteristics of brightness, activity and inertia; it is embodied in the elements and the senses and it serves the purpose of enjoyment and emancipation.

The seen, that is the material, has the characteristics of brightness, activity and inertia. These are the characteristics of Nature, or prakṛti. It serves to delight the senses and it is the vehicle that leads to emancipation or freedom.

विशेषाविशेषलिङ्गमात्रालिङ्गानि गुणपर्वाणि॥२.१९॥

viśeṣāviśeṣaliṅgamātrāliṅgāni guṇaparvāṇi ॥2.19॥

2.19 The states of the elements are the particularized, the unparticularized, the differentiate, and the undifferentiate.

Nature is unparticularized or what is potential (tanmātras) before the elements are embodied; the particularized that are the elements (the five elements) that constitute different kinds of matter; the undifferentiate matter and the differentiate matter with complex characteristics.

द्रष्टा दृशिमात्रः शुद्धोऽपि प्रत्ययानुपश्यः॥२.२०॥

draṣṭā dṛśimātraḥ śuddho'pi pratyayānupaśyaḥ ॥2.20॥

2.20 The seer who is one with the power of seeing is pure and he perceives the ideas by causes.

Although the power of seeing is in the seer, the actual cognition is made by inference from the causes.

तदर्थ एव दृश्यस्यात्मा ॥२.२१॥

tadartha eva dṛśyasyātmā ॥2.21॥

2.21 The essence of the seen is only for the sake of the seer.

The phenomenal universe with the embodiment of all that can be seen is for the sake of the seer. In other words, the embodiment is an act of consciousness.

कृतार्थं प्रति नष्टम् अप्यनष्टं तदन्यसाधारणत्वात् ॥२.२२॥

kṛtārthaṃ prati naṣṭaṃ apyanaṣṭaṃ tadanyasādhāraṇatvāt ॥2.22॥

2.22 Although it ceases to exist for one whose purpose is accomplished, the seen does not cease to exist as it is common experience to others.

At the level of the individual for whom the purpose of the seen ends after he has obtained understanding and found how it is related to the mind and saṃskāras, the reality continues to have its common form to others who have not reached this level.

स्वस्वामिशक्त्योः स्वरूपोपलब्धिहेतुः संयोगः ॥२.२३॥

svasvāmiśaktyoḥ svarūpoplabdhihetuḥ saṃyogaḥ ॥2.23॥

2.23 Coincidence or conjunction allows the apprehension of the nature of the self by the power of the self.

The seer and the seen are in a continuing state of conjunction due to the transcending nature of the puruṣa. It is this conjunction that makes it possible for the phenomenal mind to apprehend the nature of reality.

तस्य हेतुरविद्या ॥२.२४॥

tasya heturavidyā ॥2.24॥

2.24 Its effective cause is materiality.

The causal basis of coincidence is avidyā or materiality. Avidyā is sometimes seen as ignorance. It is not ignorance in the sense of lack of some specific material knowledge or knowledge of specific material processes. Avidyā is the view that the material world is closed in itself and consciousness is an epiphenomenon. Nevertheless, materiality has within it the possibility of knowing how its system is incomplete and, therefore, it can prepare one for true knowledge.

तदभावात् संयोगाभावो हानं। तद्दृशेः कैवल्यम्॥२.२५॥

Tadabhāvāt saṃyogābhāvo hānaṃ taddṛśeḥ kaivalyam ॥2.25॥

2.25 Removal is the absence of the conjunction on account of its disappearance which is the freedom of the knower.

Conjunction or coincidence which is the cause of the pain to the yogi is removed once he has found freedom. At the larger level, there is likewise conjunction based on natural processes, but this conjunction may not exist when the freedom of the knower is a factor. The absence of this conjunction then exhibits itself as an unexpected event or piece of knowledge that cannot be explained away.

विवेकख्यातिरविप्लवा हानोपायः॥२.२६॥

vivekakhyātiraviplavā hānopāyaḥ ॥2.26॥

2.26 The means for attaining cessation is unwavering discernment.

Unwavering discernment provides the capacity to remove the conjunctions within one's own experience. These conjunctions are like the proverbial box within which one is situated all one's life.

तस्य सप्तधा प्रान्तभूमिः प्रज्ञा॥२.२७॥

tasya saptadhā prāntabhūmiḥ prajña ॥2.27॥

2.27 For such a person arises in the last stage a seven-fold intuition.

The seven folds of intuition are listed as follows by the commentator Vyāsa: (i) painful experiences to be removed are recounted; (ii) the causes of the pain are removed; (iii) removal has become a direct cognition; (iv) the means of knowledge in terms of discrimination are understood; (v) the removal of tamas or inertia; (vi) the removal of rajas or activity; and, finally, (vii) the removal of sattva, or transparence. After this one's intuition can directly cognize events and processes.

योगाङ्गानुष्ठानाद् अशुद्धिक्षये ज्ञानदीप्तिरा विवेकख्यातेः॥२.२८॥

yogāṅgānuṣṭhānād aśuddhikṣaye jñānadīptirā vivekakhyāteḥ ॥2.28॥

2.28 By means of yoga and by destroying impurity there is enlightenment that reaches discriminative wisdom.

Impurity is the reality that is a projection of the mind and the saṃskāras.

यमनियमासनप्राणायामप्रत्याहारधारणाध्यानसमाधयोऽष्टाव अङ्गानि॥२.२९॥

yamaniyamāsanaprāṇāyāmapratyāhāradhāraṇādhyānasamādhayo'ṣṭāva aṅgāni ||2.29||

2.29 Restraint, observance, posture, breath-control, abstraction, concentration, meditation, and trance are the eight limbs of yoga.

The eight limbs of Patañjali's yoga are: the *yamas* are the restraints, the *niyamas* are the observances, the *āsana* is the posture, the *prāṇāyāma* is breath-control, the *pratyāhāra* is the abstraction or sense-withdrawal, the *dhāraṇā* or concentration, the *dhyāna* or meditation, and *samādhi* or trance.

samādhi
dhyāna
dhāraṇā
pratyāhāra
prāṇāyāma
āsana
niyama
yama

The eight stages of yoga

In the Śāṇḍilya Upaniṣad it is stated that the yamas and the niyamas are ten each, āsanas are eight in number, the prāṇāyāma is of three kind, the pratyāhāra can be done in five ways, the dhāraṇās are also five, the dhyāna is of two kinds, and samādhi is of just one kind.

अहिंसासत्यास्तेयब्रह्मचर्यापरिग्रहा यमाः॥२.३०॥

ahiṃsāsatyāsteyabrahmacaryāparigrahā yamāḥ ||2.30||

2.30 Non-injury, truth, non-stealing, chastity and greedlessness are the restraints.

Self-discipline is fundamental to progress in wisdom. This is opposite to greed and avarice that is encouraged by modernity.

Ahiṃsā, or non-injury, encourages one to find harmony with the rest of the world.

Satya, or truth, is not an abstraction but rather it is the flow of reality in its unalloyed form. *Sat* to the baseball hitter is when he can see the ball so well that it appears as large as a basketball and he can literally anticipate what the pitcher is going to throw to him.

Asteya is the abstinence of theft: this is a call to ethical behavior. A person steals when he thinks no one is watching. The restraint of non-stealing is to do only actions that are perfectly ethical and above board.

Brahmacarya, or chastity, is the path of the seeking of *Brahman*. In popular understanding it is taken to mean absence of sexual activity because such activity can mean preoccupation with the material world which is not the path of knowing *Brahman*.

Aparigraha, abstinence from avariciousness, is another element of ethical behavior.

The Śāṇḍilya Upaniṣad adds to the first four these additional six: *dayā* (kindness), *japa* (repetition of name), *kṣamā* (patience), *dhṛti* (steadfastness), *mitāhāra* (moderation in eating), and *śauca* (purity).

जातिदेशकालसमयानवच्छिन्नाः सार्वभौमा महाव्रतम् ॥२.३१॥

jātideśakālasamayānavacchinnāḥ sārvabhaumā mahāvratam ॥2.31॥

2.31 The restraints become the great vow when they are universal and unrestricted by considerations of birth, place, time or circumstance.

Our moral restraints are normally determined by circumstances of birth, place, time or circumstance. For example, the fisherman must cause injury to the fish, or the fighter on the battlefield to the enemy soldiers. Clearly a universal vow is extraordinary and very few people would be in a position to make it.

शौचसंतोषतपःस्वाध्यायेश्वरप्रणिधानानि नियमाः ॥२.३२॥

śaucasaṃtoṣatapaḥ svādhyāyeśvarapraṇidhānāni niyamāḥ ॥2.32॥

2.32 Purity, contentment, discipline, self-study and devotion to the self are the observances.

The observances that guide one's behavior go hand in hand with the restraints.

purity	contentment	discipline	svādhyāya	devotion
ahiṃsā	truth	asteya	brahmacarya	aparigraha

Yama and Niyama

The Śāṇḍilya Upaniṣad lists these ten as the observances: *tapa* (austerity), *santoṣa* (contentment), *āstikya* (faith), *dāna* (charity), *Īśvara-pūjana* (worship of the Lord), *siddhānta śravaṇa* (reflection on vedānta), *hrī* (shame in doing actions that are not sanctioned), *mati* (respect for the tradition), *japa* (repetition of names), and *vrata* (Vedic vows). We find that Śāṇḍilya lists *japa* in both the yamas and the niyamas.

The restraints and the observances go hand in hand.

वितर्कबाधने प्रतिपक्षभावनम्॥२.३३॥

vitarkabādhane pratiprakṣabhāvanam ॥2.33॥

2.33 To restrict unwholesome thoughts, their opposites should be cultivated.

The cultivation of wholesome thoughts is to counteract those currents within oneself that diminish oneself.

It is because the mind is a microcosm that mirrors the macrocosm, it consists of all opposites. Education and culture should facilitate the growth of the higher qualities at the expense of the lower ones.

Within each one of us lie both noble and base instincts. Education and yoga is also a process of transforming oneself. It is a churning of the inner ocean. On the one side lie the gods and on the other lie the asuras (demons). We need both the base and the noble to produce insight.

वितर्का हिंसादयः कृतकारितानुमोदिता लोभक्रोधमोहपूर्वका मृदुमध्याधिमात्रा दुःखाज्ञानानन्तफला इति प्रतिपक्षभावनम्॥२.३४॥

vitarkā hiṃsādayaḥ kṛtakāritānumoditā lobhakrodhamohapūrvakā mṛdumadhyādhimātrā duḥkhājñānānanta phalā iti pratiprakṣabhāvanam ॥2.34॥

2.34 Actions arising out of unwholesome thoughts like injuring someone, done, caused to be done or approved, whether arising from greed, anger or infatuation, whether modest, medium or excessive --- these find unending fruition in ignorance and sorrow; thus their opposites should be cultivated.

All processes within leave traces. Negativity begets negativity not only outside but also within.

अहिंसाप्रतिष्ठायां तत्सन्निधौ वैरत्यागः ॥२.३५॥

ahiṃsāpratiṣṭhāyāṃ tatsannidhau vairatyāghaḥ ॥2.35॥

2.35 When a person is grounded in the virtue of non-injury, others abandon enmity in his presence.

Violence is often a reaction to perceived or imagined danger. Behavior that is clearly non-injurious is disarming.

सत्यप्रतिष्ठायां क्रियाफलाश्रयत्वम्॥२.३६॥

satyapratiṣṭhāyāṃ kriyāphalāśrayatvam ॥2.36॥

2.36 When grounded in truth, action and its fruition depend on him.

If one is grounded in truth seen as *sat*, the unfolding reality, one would clearly have access to the fruit that is associated with the unfolded phase. It is in this sense that truth bears fruit invariably.

अस्तेयप्रतिष्ठायां सर्वरत्नोपस्थानम्॥२.३७॥

asteyapratiṣṭhāyāṃ sarvaratnopasthānam ॥2.37॥

2.37 When grounded in non-stealing, all jewels appear to him.

When the yogi's moral principles are firmly established, people trust him with their most valuable things. The word jewel (*ratna*) is not to be taken literally.

ब्रह्मचर्यप्रतिष्ठायां वीर्यलाभः॥२.३८॥

brahmacaryapratiṣṭhāyāṃ vīryalābhaḥ ॥2.38॥

2.38 When grounded in chastity, vitality is acquired.

The word that is usually taken to mean *chastity* is *brahmacarya*. This word *brahmacarya* means one who is living on the path of *brahman*, the world-force. Being on this path one is in harmony with the unfoldment of events and thus his vitality is strengthened by individuals and things around him.

अपरिग्रहस्थैर्ये जन्मकथंतासंबोधः ॥२.३९॥

aparigrahasthairye janmakathaṃtāsaṃbodhaḥ ॥2.39॥

2.39 When steadied in greedlessness, he perceives the reasons for his birth.

Vyāsa says that as a person is confirmed in non-covetousness, he starts meditating on who he is, where he has come from, and so on, which eventually yields answers to these questions.

शौचात् स्वाङ्गजुगुप्सा परैरसंसर्गः ॥२.४०॥

śaucāt svāṅgajugupsā parairasaṃsargaḥ ॥2.40॥

2.40 By purity he gains a separation from his limbs as also a desire for distance from others.

By stressing purity, the yogi becomes aware of his own imperfections and impurities. This makes it easy to separate his essential self from that of his body and also that of other bodies since they are as impure as his own body.

सत्त्वशुद्धिसौमनस्यैकाग्र्येन्द्रियजयात्मदर्शनयोग्यत्वानि च ॥२.४१॥

sattvaśuddhisaumanasyaikāgryendriyajayātmadarśanayogyatvāni ca ॥2.41॥

2.41 Purity of the mind, gladness, one-pointedness, mastery of the senses and the capacity for self-realization are then achieved.

As the yogi is confirmed in purity, gladness or high-mindedness, mastery of the sense, and capacity for self-realization are achieved in succession.

संतोषाद् अनुत्तमः सुखलाभः ॥२.४२॥

saṃtoṣād anuttamaḥ sukhalābhaḥ ॥2.42॥

2.42 By contentment unexcelled joy is gained.

Contentment sets in motion a series of further developments mentioned earlier that lead to the bliss of *Brahman* which is greater than any other bliss (as stressed by Taittirīya and other Upaniṣads).

कायेन्द्रियसिद्धिरशुद्धिक्षयात् तपसः ॥२.४३॥

kāyendriyasiddhiraśuddhikṣayāt tapasaḥ ॥2.43॥

2.43 By discipline, on account of the dwindling of impurity, perfection of body and senses is gained.

As one identifies with the pure, impurity dwindles. This is akin to what neuroscientists have observed in that the centers of brain devoted to specific action performed by the individual increase in size at the expense of others. We become what we think and do and identify with. As we identify with purity, we become more pure.

स्वाध्यायाद् इष्टदेवतासंप्रयोगः ॥२.४४॥

Svādhyāyād iṣṭadevatāsaṃprayogaḥ ॥2.44॥

2.44 Through self-study contact with the chosen deity is attained.

By means of self-study (*svādhyāya*) one gets to know one's own essential temperament which makes it clear who one's chosen deity should be since this deity should be consonant with this temperament.

समाधिसिद्धिरीश्वरप्रणिधानात्॥२.४५॥

samādhisiddhirīśvarapraṇidhānāt ॥2.45॥

2.45 Through devotion to the self comes that attainment of perfect concentration.

The sūtra speaks of devotion to *Īśvara* (the Lord, enjoyer) which we have translated as *self.* Since the mind is an artifact of our circumstances and history, the real *self* is the same for everyone and he is *Īśvara*. When absorbed in the real self, all other distractions fall away.

स्थिरसुखम् आसनम्॥२.४६॥

Sthirasukham āsanam ॥2.46॥

2.46 Posture should be steady and comfortable.

Vyāsa lists many āsanas that were considered steady and comfortable. He speaks of the following āsanas: Padmāsana, Vīrāsana, Bhadrāsana, Svastika, Daṇḍāsana, Sopaśraya, Paryaṅka, Krauñcaniṣadana, Hastīniṣadana, Uṣṭraniṣadana, Samasaṃsthāna, Sthirasukha, Yathāsukha, and says there are others. This confirms that very many āsanas were being practiced in the earliest times. These āsanas are described in words by Vācaspati.

Several āsanas are described in the Triśikha-brāhmaṇa-Upaniṣad. Śāṇḍilya names his eight āsanas to be Svastika, Gomukha, Padma, Vīra,

Siṃha, [Siddha], Bhadra, Mukta, and Mayūra and these are described in detail.

प्रयत्नशैथिल्यानन्तसमापत्तिभ्याम् ॥२.४७॥

prayatnaśaithilyānantasamāpattibhyām ॥2.47॥

2.47 [It is accompanied with] relaxation and coincidence with the infinite.

Vācaspati explains: "The effort which is directed to the holding of the āsana (posture) keeps the body in that position. It is not the cause of the āsana, for if that were its cause the teaching would be useless in the sense that the posture will be achieved by its own effort. The natural effort of the body does not bring about the posture; it is in fact its antagonistic. This natural effort being the antecedent of the posture does away with the very object of the posture. Therefore one who does the āsana should employ an effort which suppresses the natural tendency of the body."

ततो द्वन्द्वानभिघातः ॥२.४८॥

tato dvaṅdvānabhighātaḥ ॥2.48॥

2.48 Thence unassailability by paired opposites.

When the āsana has been mastered the yogi is not affected by opposites such as heat and cold or the opposites associated with the mind and its contents.

तस्मिन् सति श्वासप्रश्वासयोर्गतिविच्छेदः प्राणायामः ॥२.४९॥

tasmin sati śvāsapraśvāsyorgativicchedaḥ prāṇāyāmaḥ ॥2.49॥

2.49 The next step is prāṇāyāma (breath control), which is the breaking of the flow of inhalation and exhalation.

Vācaspati explains that *prāṇāyāma* is the cessation of the movements of inhalation and exhalation in *recaka* (cessation of breath after exhalation), *pūraka* (cessation of breath after inhalation), and *kumbhaka* (both these cessations). The differences in recaka, pūraka, and kumbhaka define the three kinds of prāṇāyāma.

Śāṇḍilya advises that at the end of pūraka one should perform the jālandhara bandha (the throat lock) and in recaka and kumbhaka the uḍḍiyāṇa bandha (the solar plexus lock).

According to Śāṇḍilya and the Gorakṣa Paddhati, prāṇāyāma is the joining of prāṇa and apāna, which are dominant above and below the navel, respectively.

बाह्याभ्यन्तरस्तम्भवृत्तिः देशकालसंख्याभिः परिदृष्टो दीर्घसूक्ष्मः ॥२.५०॥

bāhyābhyantarasthambhavṛttiḥ deśakālasankhyābhiḥ paridṛṣṭo dīrghasūkṣmaḥ ॥2.50॥

2.50 Breath control is external, internal and fixed in its movement; it is regulated by place, time and number; it is protracted or contracted.

The control of breath can be done in terms of place, unit of time considered, and the number of these units used.

बाह्याभ्यन्तरविषयाक्षेपी चतुर्थः ॥२.५१॥

bāhyābhyantara viṣayākṣepī caturthaḥ ॥2.51॥

2.51 The fourth movement of the breath transcends internal and external spheres.

The details of how these movements of prāṇāyāma are made vary from school to school as evidenced by the different views of the commentators. These details depend on how advanced the yogi is in his practice.

Śāṇḍilya explains that the purpose of prāṇāyāma is the purification and control of the nerves of the body. He speaks of the place of the *kuṇḍalinī* at the bottom of the spine. From there rise fourteen major nerves: *iḍā, piṅgalā, suṣumnā, sarasvatī, vāruṇī, pūṣā, hastajivā, yaśasvinī, viśvodarī, kuhū, śaṅkhinī, payasvinī, alambusā,* and *gāndhārī.* The same list is also found in Jābāla-Darśana-Upaniṣad.

The *suṣumnā* is the pathway to deepest intuition; to its left is iḍā, whose characteristics are according to that of the moon, and to its right is piṅgalā, which moves according to the sun. Behind *suṣumnā* is *sarasvatī* that goes all the way to the tip of the tongue; kuhū is at the place of the genitalia, and śaṅkhinī is at the anus. It is part of beginning practice to get familiar with each of these fourteen nerves. The suṣumnā is also called rākā.

In these nerves course ten different breaths: *prāṇa, apāna, samāna, udāna, vyāna, nāga, kūrma, kṛkara, devadatta,* and *dhanañjaya.* Of these the prāṇa moves through mouth, nose, throat, navel, the big toes, and the kuṇḍalinī; the apāna courses through the genitalia and the navel and it establishes heat; the samāna is the current that courses through feet, hands, and the organs; the udāna is the prāṇa that is present at conjunction points from where 72,000 other nerves arise; and the vyāna moves through ears, eyes, waist, elbow, nose, throat, and hips. The next four breaths are present in eructation (nāga), blinking of eyes (kūrma), hunger (kṛkara), and yawning and sleep (devadatta); the last, dhananjaya, is the breath that is responsible for the disintegration of the dead organism.

Clearly, the practice of prāṇāyāma requires control of each of these breaths in the body and doing so provides control over the nervous system.

Most importantly, the play between prāṇa and apāna represents the practice of prāṇāyāma.

By the practice of prāṇāyāma, the practitioner becomes familiar with the seven cakras: mūlādhāra at the bottom of the spine, svādhiṣṭhāna, maṇipūra at the navel, anāhata at the heart, viśuddha at the throat, ājña between the eyes, and the sahasrāra at the crown of the head.

ततः क्षीयते प्रकाशावरणम्॥२.५२॥

tataḥ kṣīyate prakāśāvaraṇam ॥2.52॥

2.52 Thence the covering of the inner light disappears.

The covering of the inner light is what separates the individual from the truth within. The mastering of prāṇāyāma sets in motion a variety of changes that allows the person to transcend the chain of karma and become free and have access to the light within.

धारणासु च योग्यता मनसः॥२.५३॥

dhāraṇāsu ca yogyatā manasaḥ ॥2.53॥

2.53 The mind is prepared for fixed attention.

The inner light is much more powerful than outer distractions and, therefore, the yogi is prepared for dhāraṇā concentration.

स्वविषयासंप्रयोगे चित्तस्य स्वरूपानुकार इवेन्द्रियाणां प्रत्याहारः॥२.५४॥
svaviṣayāsaṃprayoge cittasya svarūpānukāra ivendriyāṇāṃ pratyāhāraḥ ॥2.54॥

2.54 When separated from objects, the senses follow the nature of the mind – that is pratyāhāra or sense withdrawal.

It is the nature of the mind to fill itself with whatever objects it is offered. When the mind is separated from objects, it is able to withdraw from the senses.

According to Śāṇḍilya the five varieties of pratyāhāra are: drawing in of the senses, seeing all as ātman, sacrificing fruits of action, turning away from sense gratification, and control over the eighteen nerve centers of the body from the toe to the head. Such pratyāhāra becomes possible through the practice of prāṇāyāma only after the practitioner first learns to recognize these centers by means of their specific prāṇas and then learns to control them.

ततः परमा वश्यतेन्द्रियाणाम्॥२.५५॥

tataḥ paramā vaśyatendriyāṇām ॥2.55॥

2.55 Thence arises supreme mastery of the senses.

As the mind withdraws from the senses, it masters them. Separating the mind and the senses spontaneously makes it possible for the mind to control the senses.

इति पतञ्जलिविरचिते योगसूत्रे द्वितीयः साधनपादः।

Here ends the second part of Patañjali's Yoga-sūtra on the means of attainment.

3. Extraordinary Powers

तृतीयः विभूतिपादः

देशबन्धश्चित्तस्य धारणा॥३.१॥

deśabandhaścittasya dhāraṇā ॥3.1॥

3.1 Concentration or dhāraṇā is the steadfastness of the mind.

Steadfastness is the binding of the mind to the place within the body. One cannot concentrate on a subject by an effort of will for the mind would wander to other topics and places. Any subject is also not a localized thing because by its nature it has extension and characteristics. The way to concentrate, therefore, is to fix the gaze of the mind to a specific location within the body such as the navel, the forehead, or some other part. What such concentration does is to make the nerves *pure*, that is to suppress the natural noise associated with pathways of the body and localize the aggregated activity in the nerves.

The purification of the nerves could begin by efforts at obtaining control of isolated muscles in the body.

Concentration (dhāraṇā), therefore, is associated firstly with the inner body and only after that is properly mapped does one obtain the facility of concentrating on outer objects. This means that concentration is the first step in the discovery of the inner world.

Śāṇḍilya speaks of three kinds of dhāraṇā: the visualization of the mind in the ātman, the visualization of the outer sky in the sky of the heart, and the visualization of the five deities in the five elements.

तत्र प्रत्ययैकतानता ध्यानम्॥३.२॥

tatra pratyayaikatānatā dhyānam ॥3.2॥

3.2 Continuing focusing the mental-effort on the place is meditation.

Meditation or dhyāna is thus nothing other than extended concentration. It may be outer-directed or inner-directed. The performance of the artist, which requires a very long stretch of concentration, is an example of meditation.

Śāṇḍilya says that dhyāna is of two kinds: *saguṇa* or with attributes and *nirguṇa*, that is without attributes.

तद् एवार्थमात्रनिर्भासं स्वरूपशून्यम् इव समाधिः॥३.३॥

Tada evārthamātranirbhāsaṃ svarūpaśūnyam iva samādhiḥ ॥3.3॥

3.3 Meditation, shining forth as the object alone, is trance or samādhi.

In samādhi the individual does not interpose himself between the object and its cognition. In other words, the individual loses his sense of self or being there and he flows with the activity. In samādhi, man and nature are one.

Sometimes dhyāna and samādhi are described somewhat in an overlapping manner and samādhi itself is taken to be saguṇa or nirguṇa.

त्रयम् एकत्र संयमः॥३.४॥

Trayam ekatra saṃyamaḥ ॥3.4॥

3.4 The three together constitute restraint.

Concentration, meditation, and samādhi taken together are called saṃyama or what we call restraint. It is clearly not restraint in the sense of stopping something but, rather, the entire process that leads to samādhi. In other words, saṃyama makes it possible to have control over the process of samādhi.

तज्जयात् प्रज्ञाऽऽलोकः॥३.५॥

tajjayāt prajñā''lokaḥ ॥3.5॥

3.5 From that is born intuitive insight.

Insight is obtained by means of restraint on the object of cognition. Intuitive insight is born out of the process of losing awareness of one's own self. Restraint or saṃyama is the way to develop intuition.

This idea of deliberate development of intuition is different from how intuition is ordinarily considered. It is acknowledged that each individual has a unique intuition but what it is and how it is arrived at is left unstated or unexamined. Scientists, writers, politicians and others are guided ultimately by their intuition that trumps what experts say. The process of finding a leader is to let people with good intuition rise up through their actions. In the yogic way, there is the possibility for everyone to develop their intuition.

तस्य भूमिषु विनियोगः ॥३.६॥

tasya bhūmiṣu viniyogaḥ ॥3.6॥

3.6 It is grounded in gradual progression.

The progression of intuition occurs through a series of planes of cognition. Yoga is a process of deeper insights. At the deepest level of the mind is the flame of consciousness.

त्रयम् अन्तरङ्गं पूर्वेभ्यः ॥३.७॥

trayam antaraṅgaṃ pūrvebhyaḥ ॥3.7॥

3.7 The three limbs (namely concentration, meditation, and samādhi) are deeper in succession.

The definition of a hierarchical sequence indicates that samādhi itself leads to a still deeper cognition that is entirely beyond words. This indicates that the deeper level represents a deeper plane of experience and reality.

तद् अपि बहिरङ्गं निर्बीजस्य ॥३.८॥

tad api bahiraṅgaṃ nirbījasya ॥3.8॥

3.8 Yet they are outer limbs to seedless concentration.

Beyond the three lies seedless concentration which is beyond words. The seed concentration is what can be described in conceptual terms.

व्युत्थाननिरोधसंस्कारयोरभिभवप्रादुर्भावौ निरोधक्षणचित्तान्वयो निरोधपरिणामः ॥३.९॥

vyutthānanirodhasaṃskārayorabhibhavaprādurbhāvau nirodhakṣaṇacittānvayo nirodhapariṇāmaḥ ॥3.9॥

3.9 When there is suppression of the emergence of saṃskāras and a manifestation of the impressions of constraint, this is the restriction transformation connected with the mind in its moment of restriction.

The process of the emergence of seedless concentration is preceded by a balance with the modifications of the mind.

तस्य प्रशान्तवाहिता संस्कारात्॥३.१०॥

tasya praśāntavāhitā saṃskārat ॥3.10॥

3.10 The saṃskāras provide its undisturbed flow.

The saṃskāras obtained by the practice of restraint make it possible for the unfoldment of the state in an undisturbed manner.

It is paradoxical that the attempt to undo the effects of our early saṃskāras is to create new saṃskāras. The mind needs to destroy itself to create a new mind just like Śiva's ceaseless dance of destruction and creation. Eventually, it is not to a specific part of the dance that the performance leads, but the dance itself has within it its meaning.

सर्वार्थतैकाग्रतयोः क्षयोदयौ चित्तस्य समाधिपरिणामः॥३.११॥

sarvārthataikāgrātayoḥ kṣayodayau cittasya samādhipariṇāmaḥ ॥3.11॥

3.11 The dwindling of dispersiveness and the rise of one-pointedness is the transformation of the mind to perfect samādhi.

Samādhi is a result of the destruction of all-pointedness and the rise of one-pointedness. Our ordinary consciousness is all-pointed and in a state of chaotic unfolding. Samādhi makes our consciousness one-pointed, which is a point that was made also in an earlier sūtra.

ततः पुनः शान्तोदितौ तुल्यप्रत्ययौ चित्तस्यैकाग्रतापरिणामः॥३.१२॥

tataḥ punaḥ śāntoditau tulyapratyayau cittasyaikāgratāpariṇāmaḥ ॥3.12॥

3.12 Then again, when cognitions presented by the quiescent and the uprisen are similar, this is the transformation that makes the mind one-pointed.

One-pointedness requires that the rising and subsiding cognitions be similar. Another way to look at this is to see that our ordinary cognitions are a consequence of the disparity that lies between the mind's outer and inner skies. When the two have become identical, one is in the state of one-pointedness.

एतेन भूतेन्द्रियेषु धर्मलक्षणावस्थापरिणामा व्याख्याताः॥३.१३॥

etena bhūtendriyeṣu dharmalakṣaṇāvasthāpariṇāmā vyākhyātāḥ ॥3.13॥

3.13 By this are also explained the transformations of form, time-variation and state with regard to the elements and the senses.

This explains how the characteristic, secondary qualities and condition in the object and the senses go through changes.

शान्तोदिताव्यपदेश्यधर्मानुपाती धर्मी ॥३.१४॥

śāntoditāvyapadeśyadharmānupātī dharmī ॥3.14॥

3.14 The object characterized is defined by its quiescent, uprisen and indeterminable qualities.

The characterization of the object is in terms of differentiates based on capacity.

क्रमान्यत्वं परिणामान्यत्वे हेतुः ॥३.१५॥

kramānyatvaṃ pariṇāmānyatve hetuḥ ॥3.15॥

3.15 The distinctness of succession is the reason for the difference in transformations.

If the end states of a series of transformations are different that is because their intermediate succession states were different.

परिणामत्रयसंयमाद् अतीतानागतज्ञानम् ॥३.१६॥

pariṇāmatrayasaṃyamād atītānāgatajñānam ॥3.16॥

3.16 Through constraint (saṃyama) on the three transformations comes the knowledge of the past and the future.

If one were to define the beginning, intermediate and final states, one can extrapolate earlier and future states. This further means that, in principle, systems can be completely described. This is, of course, at the basis of ordinary science also.

शब्दार्थप्रत्ययानाम् इतरेतराध्यासात् संकरः। तत्प्रविभागसंयमात् सर्वभूतरुतज्ञानम् ॥३.१७॥

Śabdārthapratyayāmām itaretarādhyāsāt saṃkaraḥ। tatpravibhāgasaṃyamāt sarvabhūtarutajñānam ॥3.17॥

3.17 The word, the idea, and the object are confused when they are identified with each other. Through constraint (saṃyama) upon the distinction of these one acquires the knowledge of the properties of all elements.

In naïve narrative, the word, the idea, and the object are often used interchangeably. Upon a deeper reflection on the three, the distinctions between them become apparent.

संस्कारसाक्षात्करणात् पूर्वजातिज्ञानम्॥३.१८॥

saṃskārasākṣātkaraṇāt pūrvajātijñānam ||3.18||

3.18 Through direct perception of saṃskāras there comes the knowledge of the previous class.

The previous class is sometimes taken to be a previous birth. This sūtra merely generalizes what is true of objects in general to life. Thus unfoldment by natural law applies not only to the inanimate world but also to living and sentient beings.

प्रत्ययस्य परचित्तज्ञानम्॥३.१९॥

pratyayasya paracittajñānam ||3.19||

3.19 Through saṃyama on ideas, there comes knowledge of another mind.

The objects of the mind of individuals follow laws just like other objects. Thus it is possible to understand other minds.

By this analysis, once it is recognized that the mind is an instrument like other instruments it is also realized that the mind in itself does not impart uniqueness to the individual.

Suffering arises out of our attachment to the mind and to the idea that it is unique and precious. Well it is unique and precious but only due to its history and not due to anything that is permanent within it.

It is the sense of the uniqueness of the mind that one fills self-pity and resentment with the world.

न च तत् सालम्बनं तस्याविषयी भूतत्वात् ॥३.१९a॥

na ca tat sālambanaṃ tasyāviṣayī bhūtatvāt ||3.19a||

But the underlying ground of that knowledge remains out of reach.

This is so since one can only know the other mind for a brief period and to go into its heart will require becoming the other person.

कायरूपसंयमात् तद्ग्राह्यशक्तिस्तम्भे चक्षुःप्रकाशासंप्रयोगेऽन्तर्धानम्॥३.२०॥

kāyarūpasaṃyamāt tadgrāhyaśaktistambhe cakṣuḥ
prakāśāsaṃprayoge'ntardhānam ॥3.20॥

3.20 By saṃyama on the form of the body, upon the suspension of the capacity to be perceived, that is to say upon the disruption of the light traveling to the eye, there follows invisibility.

This indicates that the process that makes the body visible is one that lends itself to scientific knowledge. If the light rays that make an object recognizable are disrupted by some means, then the object will become invisible.

But the basis or prop of that idea does not get known because that is not in the field of consciousness. Making something invisible is a consequence of control over material processes.

सोपक्रमं निरुपक्रमं च कर्म। तत्संयमाद् अपरान्तज्ञानम्, अरिष्टेभ्यो वा॥३.२१॥

sopakramaṃ nirupakramaṃ ca karma। tatsaṃyamād aparāntajñānam
ariṣṭebhyo vā ॥3.21॥

3.21 Karma is of two kinds: acute or deferred. Through saṃyama thereon or from other signs (portents) one acquires knowledge of death.

There are two kinds of processes: fast and slow. One normally does not take note of the slow processes which can provide clues to death.

मैत्र्यादिषु बलानि॥३.२२॥

maitryādiṣu balāni ॥3.22॥

3.22 By saṃyama on friendliness, one acquires strength.

Friendliness, compassion, and sympathy disarm people and opens way to success, which is equivalent to strength.

बलेषु हस्तिबलादीनि॥३.२३॥

baleṣu hastibalādīni ॥3.23॥

3.23By saṃyama on strength, one knows elephant's strength.

By analysis of what gives strength to the elephant, one can replicate this strength in oneself and in one's creations.

प्रवृत्त्यालोकन्यासात् सूक्ष्मव्यवहितविप्रकृष्टज्ञानम्॥३.२४॥

pravṛttyālokanyāsāt sūkṣmāvyavahitaviprakṛṣṭajñānam ||3.24||

3.24 By applying the effulgent light of the senses, knowledge of subtle, concealed and distant objects is gained.

Knowledge of distant or subtle objects is obtained because the world consists of interconnected processes. We can obtain this knowledge by direct observation or by inference.

भुवनज्ञानं सूर्ये संयमात्॥३.२५॥

bhuvanajñānaṃ sūrye saṃyamāt ||3.25||

3.25 By saṃyama on the sun, knowledge of the world is gained.

The sun provides energy to the earth and the motions of the planets and the moon help us keep track of time. Our world, on earth, is based on the energy that is obtained through sunlight and the way time is fashioned by the motion of the earth around the sun.

चन्द्रे ताराव्यूहज्ञानम्॥३.२६॥

candre tāravyūhajñānam ||3.26||

3.26 [By saṃyama] on the moon, knowledge of the arrangement of the stars [is gained].

Understanding the motion of the moon around the earth, which is the easiest to notice, will lead to an understanding of laws that also govern the motions of stars.

ध्रुवे तद्गतिज्ञानम्॥३.२७॥

dhruve tadgatijñānam ||3.27||

3.27 [By saṃyama] on the pole star, knowledge of the motion of the stars [is gained].

नाभिचक्रे कायव्यूहज्ञानम्॥३.२८॥

nābhicakre kāyavyūhajñānam ||3.28||

3.28 [By saṃyama] on the navel plexus, knowledge of the arrangement of the body [is gained].

According to Bhoja Rāja the navel is the root of the nāḍīs, subtle nerves, which pervade the body.

कण्ठकूपे क्षुत्पिपासानिवृत्तिः ॥३.२९॥

kaṇṭhakūpe kṣutpipāsā nivṛttiḥ ॥3.29॥

3.29 [By saṃyama] on the throat-well, cessation of hunger and thirst [is gained].

Vijñānabhikṣu takes the throat-well to extend from the base of the tongue to the stomach.

Hunger and thirst are related to mental states which are clear from the behavior of people who eat and drink without control.

कूर्मनाड्यां स्थैर्यम् ॥३.३०॥

kūrmanāḍyāṃ sthairyam ॥3.30॥

3.30 [By saṃyama] on the tortoise duct, steadiness [is gained].

Vyāsa explains that the *kūrma nāḍī* (tortoise duct) is the tortoise-shaped structure below the throat pit that controls steadiness. Normally, the sense of balance is provided by the proprioception sense, which is composed of information from sensory neurons located in the inner ear (motion and orientation) and in the stretch receptors located in the muscles and the joint-supporting ligaments. The proprioceptive sense can be sharpened through training. Some people believe that the phantom limb phenomenon is a consequence of proprioceptive memory.

मूर्धज्योतिषि सिद्धदर्शनम् ॥३.३१॥

mūrdhajyotiṣi siddhadarśanam ॥3.31॥

3.31 [By saṃyama] on the light in the head, vision of the perfected beings [is gained].

This light is taken to be concentrated at the opening at the top of the skull, which is the *brahma-randhra*. This opening is likened by Bhoja Rāja to a key-hole through which one can see people in a room. The flow of light and energy takes place along the spinal cord.

प्रातिभाद् वा सर्वम्॥३.३२॥

Prātibhād vā sarvam ||3.32||

3.32 By intuition, all [is gained].

Intuition (*prātibha*) is like the dawn that precedes the light of the sun. It is called *tāraka*, by which one swims over to the shore of knowledge.

Knowledge could not be in terms of words because then it would be restricted to objects alone. The objective of yoga is to obtain knowledge related to consciousness.

हृदये चित्तसंवित्॥३.३३॥

hr̥daye cittasaṃvit ||3.33||

3.33 [By saṃyama] on the heart, the nature of the mind [is known].

The heart (*hr̥daya*) is taken by Vyāsa to be the "city of Brahman, a lotus-like abode." It is not the physical heart and it is here that intelligence resides. We are speaking here of intelligence that manifests itself through intuition. Finally, this intuition gets translated into action or expression through the faculties associated with the brain.

सत्त्वपुरुषयोरत्यन्तासंकीर्णयोः प्रत्ययाविशेषो भोगः परार्थत्वात् स्वार्थसंयमात् पुरुषज्ञानम्॥३.३४॥

sattvapuruṣayoratyantāsaṃkīrṇayoḥ pratyayāviśeṣo bhogaḥ parārthatvāt svārthasaṃyamāt puruṣajñānam ||3.34||

3.34 Experience as an idea does not distinguish between the absolutely pure self and transparence. Through constraint on the self's own purpose, which is distinct from other purposiveness, knowledge of the self is obtained.

Ordinary experience confounds the pure self with the workings of intelligence. According to Vyāsa, we see intelligence only through the mutual workings of the guṇas entangled with each other. Only when we can see the workings of *sattva* by itself can we understand puruṣa.

Vācaspati explains this well: It may be said that experience is the feeling of pleasure and pain which is in consonance or dissonance with the prevailing mental state. This cannot be in consonance or dissonance with itself. No self-contradictory manifestation can exist in itself. Hence it must be that the objects are either in consonance or dissonance and it is this that constitutes experience. The self is the enjoyer; the knowable is that which he enjoys.

ततः प्रातिभश्रावणवेदनादर्शास्वादवार्ता जायन्ते॥३.३५॥

tataḥ prātibhasrāvāṇavedanādarśāsvādavārtā jāyante ॥3.35॥

3.35 Thence are produced intuition and sharpening of the powers of hearing, sensing, sight, taste and smell.

Strengthened by his practice, the yogi gains access to subtle powers of the senses. It is through this subtle knowledge of prakṛti that his self-realization becomes possible.

ते समाधाव् उपसर्गा। व्युत्थाने सिद्धयः॥३.३६॥

te samādhāv upasargā। vyutthāne siddhayaḥ ॥3.36॥

3.36 They are impediments to concentration, but are attainments in the waking state.

These powers (*siddhis*) cause wonder and pleasure and are desirable accomplishments in normal interactions. But they are obstacles to further concentration.

बन्धकारणशैथिल्यात् प्रचारसंवेदनाच् च चित्तस्य परशरीरावेशः॥३.३७॥

badnhakāraṇaśaithilyāt pracārasaṃvedanāc ca cittasya paraśarīrāveśaḥ ॥3.37॥

3.37 By the weakening of attachment and by instruction and empathy, the mind enters another body.

This power has been taken to be literally true by many scholars. It is to be taken as the capacity to understand how others live and act, that is to understand their mind. A mind can take over another body as happens in mass hysteria. But such a capacity is also at work in more benign situations in the world that are considered normal.

The purpose of the education system and the media is to self-consciously enter the minds of different individuals.

उदानजयाज्जलपङ्ककण्टकादिष्वसङ्ग उत्क्रान्तिश्च॥३.३८॥

udānajayājjalapaṅkakaṇṭakādiṣvasaṅga utkrāntiśca ॥3.38॥

3.38 By mastery of the up-breath, one gains the power of non-adhesion to water, mud and thorns and the power to rise.

By the udāna vital air one feels light. But this is not to mean actual physical levitation.

समानजयात् प्रज्वलनम्॥३.३९॥

Samānajayāt prajvalanam ॥3.39॥

3.39 By mastery of mid-breath, one acquires radiance.

Radiance is a consequence of the *fire* burning in the body. The mid-breath (*samāna*) distributes this fire all over the body. This distribution and the effect of the other breaths occur as the mastery over the nāḍīs (nerves) increases and thus one obtains a mindful relationship with the body.

श्रोत्राकाशयोः संबन्धसंयमाद् दिव्यं श्रोत्रम्॥३.४०॥

śrotrākāśayoḥ saṃbandhasaṃyamād divyaṃ śrotram ॥3.40॥

3.40 By saṃyama on the relation between hearing and ether, one acquires divine hearing.

Divine hearing is the hearing within the inner sky which is associated with the process of intuitive understanding.

कायाकाशयोः संबन्धसंयमाल् लघुतूलसमापत्तेश्चाकाशगमनम्॥३.४१॥

kāyākāśayoḥ saṃbandhasaṃyamāl laghutūlasamāpatteścākāśagamanam ॥3.41॥

3.41 By saṃyama on the relation between body and ether and by coincidence with light objects like cotton, one obtains the powers of traversing the sky.

The possibility that one can fly was stated several centuries before it was made possible by machines.

बहिरकल्पिता वृत्तिर्महाविदेहा। ततः प्रकाशावरणक्षयः॥३.४२॥

bahirakalpitā vṛttirmahāvidehā। tataḥ prakāśāvaraṇakṣayaḥ ॥3.42॥

3.42 External formless fluctuation of the mind is the great incorporeal from which comes the dwindling of the coverings of the inner light.

According to Bhoja Rāja it is the false ego, ahaṃkāra, identifying the self with the body, which causes the individual to be confined to the body.

Practice that conceptualizes travel out of the body also weakens the false ego that facilitates the removal of the coverings of the inner light.

स्थूलस्वरूपसूक्ष्मान्वयार्थवत्त्वसंयमाद्भूतजयः ॥३.४३॥

sthūlasvarūpasūkṣmānvayārthavattvasaṃyamādbhūtajayaḥ ॥3.43॥

3.43 By saṃyama on the elemental, the self, the subtle, the relations and the goals, one gains mastery over the elements.

This is what one set out to do, to master the elements so that their distorting lens can be removed in our experience of reality.

ततोऽणिमादिप्रादुर्भावः कायसंपत् तद्धर्मानभिघातश्च ॥३.४४॥

tato'ṇimādiprādurbhāvaḥ kāyasaṃpat taddharmānabhighātaśca ॥3.44॥

3.44 Then manifest atomization etc, perfection of the body and the indestructibility of its constituents.

Mastery endows one with mystical powers and perfection of the body's capacities. The atomization is also related to the subtle control over one's own nerve systems.

रूपलावण्यबलवज्रसंहननत्वानि कायसंपत्॥३.४५॥

rūpalāvaṇyabalavajrasaṃhananatvāni kāyasaṃpat ॥3.45॥

3.45 Beauty, grace and adamant robustness constitute the perfection of the body.

The power that one obtains is compared to that of the thunderbolt. Body language mirrors inner states of the mind and the yogi's demeanor expresses a sense of beauty, confidence, and grace.

ग्रहणस्वरूपास्मितान्वयार्थवत्त्वसंयमाद् इन्द्रियजयः॥३.४६॥

grahaṇasvarūpāsmitānvayārthavattvasaṃyamād indriyajayaḥ ॥3.46॥

3.46 By saṃyama on perception, the self form, ego, relations and purposiveness, one gains mastery over the senses.

There then occurs a shift from *grahaṇa* (seizing knowledge), *svarūpa* (essence), *asmitā* (I-am-ness), *anvaya* (the three guṇas, inherent quality), to *arthavattva* (purposefulness) that is to experience liberation to puruṣa.

ततो मनोजवित्वं विकरणभावः प्रधानजयश्च॥३.४७॥

tato manojavitvaṃ vikaraṇabhāvaḥ pradhānajayaśca ॥3.47॥

3.47 Thence comes fleetness of the mind, extra-body states, and mastery over the primary cause.

The yogi now has access to additional powers. From a social point of view, the yogi has surprising accomplishments.

सत्त्वपुरुषान्यताख्यातिमात्रस्य सर्वभावाधिष्ठातृत्वं सर्वज्ञातृत्वं च॥३.४८॥

sattvapuruṣānyatākhyātimātrasya sarvabhāvādhiṣṭhātṛtvaṃ sarvajñātṛtvaṃ ca ॥3.48॥

3.48 One who has only the vision of the distinction between transparence and the self gains supremacy over all states and omniscience.

This is a state that Vyāsa calls *vaśīkāra*. The powers that the yogi obtains can be put to change the unfoldment of events.

तद्वैराग्यादपि दोषबीजक्षये कैवल्यम्॥३.४९॥

tadvairāgyādapi doṣabījakṣaye kaivalyam ॥3.49॥

3.49 By dispassion towards even this vision, with the dwindling of the seeds of the defects, one attains ultimate liberation.

The previous states were related to sabīja-samādhi that is contingent on conceptualization. But for ultimate liberation one must go to nirbīja samādhi that is beyond conceptualization.

स्थान्युपनिमन्त्रणे सङ्गस्मयाकरणं पुनः अनिष्टप्रसङ्गात्॥३.५०॥

sthānyupanimantraṇe saṅgasmayākaraṇaṃ punaḥ aniṣṭaprasaṅgāt ॥3.50॥

3.50 There should be no attachment or pride when invited by the masters because that can lead to renewed and undesired inclinations.

According to Vyāsa, there are four kinds of yogis: the beginners (*prathama kalpika*), the truth-seekers (*madhubhūmika*), the enlightened ones (*prajñājyotiḥ*), and those whose objective is to become with the cosmic mind (*atikrāntabhāvanīya*). This sūtra addresses those who are on the third stage.

क्षणतत्क्रमयोः संयमाद्विवेकजं ज्ञानम्॥३.५१॥

kṣaṇatatkramayoḥ saṃyamādvivekajaṃ jñānam ॥3.51॥

3.51 By saṃyama on the moment (kṣaṇa) and its sequence, one obtains knowledge born of discernment.

According to Vyāsa, as an atom is a substance in which minuteness reaches its limit, a moment is division of time in which minuteness reaches its limit. A moment is that much of time in which an atom reaches the next point. The aggregates of time, like muhūrta or hour, are mental conceptions, but the moment (*kṣaṇa*) has objective reality and it is maintained by succession. The yogis who know time call this by the name of time. Two moments cannot exist. The whole world undergoes change every moment and all these characteristics are established in that moment.

This view is that of the universe running according to a clock in our conception within the mind.

जातिलक्षणदेशैरन्यताऽनवच्छेदात् तुल्ययोस्ततः प्रतिपत्तिः॥३.५२॥

jātilakṣaṇadeśairanyatā'navacchedāt tulyayostataḥ pratipattiḥ ॥3.52॥

3.52 Thence arise the awareness of the difference between similar substances that cannot normally be distinguished due to an indeterminateness of the distinctions of category, appearance and position.

Distinctions arise out of difference in qualities or if the qualities are the same, differences in correlations with the rest of the world. Says Vyāsa: "By discovering the yet unknown correlation of every atomic position in space to a different moment in time, the sequential notion of such a position in space or the anterior atom becomes distinct from such a position in space for the distinction of atoms. The powerful yogi knows this distinction by the correlated moment."

तारकं सर्वविषयं सर्वथाविषयम् अक्रमं चेति विवेकजं ज्ञानम्॥३.५३॥

tārakaṃ sarvaviṣayaṃ sarvathāviṣayam akramaṃ ceti vivekajaṃ jñānam ॥3.53॥

3.54 The knowledge born of discernment is intuitional, it is comprehensive of all things and of all times, and it is non-sequential.

Discriminative knowledge cannot be obtained by teaching for it is intuitional. It is non-sequential in the sense that it is correlated with a single moment (kṣaṇa).

सत्त्वपुरुषयोः शुद्धिसाम्ये कैवल्यम् ॥३.५४॥

sattvapuruṣayoḥ śuddhisāmye kaivalyam ॥3.54॥

3.54 When the purity of transparence and the self are equal, there follows freedom.

The conceptions of the mind are a consequence of the chain of associations that words have built up. When this chain has worked through its action, one obtains absolute independence.

इति पतञ्जलिविरचिते योगसूत्रे तृतीयो विभूतिपादः।

Here ends the third part of Patañjali's Yoga-sūtra on the powers.

4. Freedom

चतुर्थः कैवल्यपादः

जन्मौषधिमन्त्रतपःसमाधिजाः सिद्धयः ॥४.१॥

janmauṣadhimantratapaḥ samādhijāḥ siddhayaḥ ॥4.1॥

4.1 Attainments are a result of birth, drugs, mantra, discipline, and meditation.

Attainments are a consequence of both nature (birth) and nurture. In nurture, we must include what we eat and what we do, and how we do it. These things affect our capacities and attainments.
The attainments by drugs are the ones favored by the Asuras or the materialists. The attainments by drugs are false peak states that lead to delusion and unhappiness.

जात्यन्तरपरिणामः प्रकृत्यापूरात्॥४.२॥

jātyantarapariṇāmaḥ prakṛtyāpūrāt ॥4.2॥

4.2 The transformation into another category is the realization of the potential.

Each successive life-state is the completion of the preceding state. This is seen most clearly in the ongoing life-state of any individual. This is true at levels beyond that of the individual's life. The analogy here is that of water that is dammed off but when the obstacles are removed it will flow down to the lower level.

It is natural then for a person to be creative and if people are not creative it is because this potential has been dammed. The obstacles in the unfolding of the potential are cause for suffering.

निमित्तम् अप्रयोजकं प्रकृतीनां। वरणभेदस्तु ततः क्षेत्रिकवत्॥४.३॥

Nimittam aprayojakaṃ prakṛtīnāṃ। varaṇabhedastu tataḥ kṣetrikavat ॥4.3॥

4.3 The incidental cause does not put Nature into motion – it merely singles out a possibility like the farmer's toil.

This argues that Nature can take many different paths and, fundamentally, there is freedom in evolution. Reality is a path in a potential of many possibilities.

The forms associated with evolution do lie as potential within the laws of prakṛti. Just as in a universe with only protons and electrons eventually the different elements will be created under appropriate conditions, the various higher forms are also implicit within Nature and they arise under appropriate conditions.

निर्माणचित्तान्यस्मितामात्रात्॥४.४॥

nirmāṇacittānyasmitāmātrāt ॥4.4॥

4.4 The individualized minds proceed from the primary ego.

Vyāsa asks the fascinating question that if a yogi makes other bodies, will these bodies have many minds or will they have just one? According to Vācaspati it will be only one mind that will pervade all the created bodies just as the light of a lamp is diffused and illuminates several bodies.

प्रवृत्तिभेदे प्रयोजकं चित्तम् एकम् अनेकेषाम्॥४.५॥

pravṛttibhede prayojakaṃ cittam ekam anekeṣām ॥4.5॥

4.5 The distinct activities (of the many) originate in the one *mind.*

What is true at the level of the creation of the yogi is true at the level of creation. This is why all sentient beings are taken to be illuminated by the same light of consciousness.

तत्र ध्यानजम् अनाशयम्॥४.६॥

tatra dhyānajam anāśayam ॥4.6॥

4.6 Of these activities those born of meditation are without deposit.

Of the attainments by birth, drugs, mantra, discipline, and meditation, it is only the one by meditation that is without the manifestation of desire.

कर्माशुक्लाकृष्णं योगिनः त्रिविधम् इतरेषाम्॥४.७॥

karmāśuklākṛṣṇaṃ yoginaḥ trividham itareṣām ॥4.7॥

4.7 The karma of the yogi is neither black nor white; that of others is of three kinds.

According to Vyāsa, actions are of four kinds: the black, the black-white, the white, and not white - not black. The black is of the wicked, the black-white is brought out by external means that cause pain to some and comfort to others. The white is that which concerns study and meditation and thus relates to the mind alone. The action which is neither black nor white relates to those who have renounced everything.

ततस्तद्विपाकानुगुणानाम् एवाभिव्यक्तिर्वासनानाम् ॥४.८॥

tatastadvipākānuguṇānām evābhivyaktirvāsanānām ॥4.8॥

4.8 Thence follow the manifestations of those traits that correspond to the fruition of the particular karma.

For those who are involved in three-fold karma (by those who are not yogis), the traits associated with the individual correspond to the action chosen. For the non-yogi life is lived essentially by conditioning and culture. But of course individuals do, due to their karmic potential, rise above their conditioning and culture to a certain extent.

जातिदेशकालव्यवहितानाम् अप्यानन्तर्यं, स्मृतिसंस्कारयोः एकरूपत्वात् ॥४.९॥

Jātideśakālavyavahitānām apyānataryaṃ smṛtisaṃskārayoḥ ekarūpatvāt ॥4.9॥

4.9 On account of similarity between memory and saṃskāras, there is causal link even if there is separation in time, place and category.

Example of this is the way genetic information manifests itself even if the seed had been held in abeyance for a long time.

तासाम् अनादित्वं चाशिषो नित्यत्वात् ॥४.१०॥

tāsām anāditvaṃ cāśiṣo nityatvāt ॥4.10॥

4.10 They are without beginning because of the perpetuity of the fundamental laws.

Vyāsa explains that there is no beginning for residua. The desire to live forever is found in everyone. How could there be fear of death and desire to avoid pain if a person has not experienced this before. The mind possessed of deep memories (residua) from eternity brings into activity only certain residua for the purpose of giving experience to Puruṣa.

Some hold that the mind attains a form that is commensurate with the body for it contracts and expands like light placed in a jar or a house. Vyāsa holds that it is the manifestation alone of the self-existing mind that expands or contracts.

हेतुफलाश्रयालम्बनैः संगृहीतत्वाद् एषाम् अभावे तदभावः ॥४.११॥

hetuphalāśrayālambanaiḥ saṃgṛhītatvād eṣām abhāve tadabhāvaḥ ॥4.11॥

4.11 Since there is a connection with cause, result, substratum and support, the disappearance of these leads to a disappearance of those [traits].

Vyāsa: The cause: by virtue comes pleasure, by vice pain. From pleasure comes attachment, from pain aversion. Thence comes effort. Acting by mind, body and speech, one either favors or injures others. Thence comes again virtue and vice, pleasure and pain, attachment and aversion. Thus revolves the six-spoked wheel of the world. The driver of this wheel is avidyā (ignorance), which is the root of the afflictions. This is the cause.

Motive or fruit is that for which appropriate virtue is harnessed. There is no non-sequential manifestation.

The substratum is the mind which has yet a duty to perform. It is there that the residua reside. They no longer reside in a mind that has already performed its action, whose substratum is gone.

The object (*ālambana*) of the residua is the substance which when placed in contact calls them forth.

Thus all residua are held together by cause, fruit, substratum, and object.

अतीतानागतं स्वरूपतोऽस्त्यध्वभेदाद् धर्माणाम्॥४.१२॥

atītānāgataṃ svarūpato'styadhvabhedād dharmāṇām ॥4.12॥

4.12 Past and future exist due to the difference in the paths of these forms.

Vyāsa: There is no existence for that which exists not, and no destruction for what exists. The future is the manifestation which is to be and the past is the appearance that has been experienced; the present is that which is in active operation.

There is no present and past in the microworld. The laws of nature are time-symmetric. Time arises out of the difference in forms in the macroworld. But even here one must admit the possibility of the cosmos going through an infinity of cycles so that at the broadest level the states of the universe are merely the many manifestations of potential.

ते व्यक्तसूक्ष्मा गुणात्मानः ॥४.१३॥

te vyaktasūkṣmā guṇātmānaḥ ॥4.13॥

4.13 These forms are manifest or subtle and composed of the primary constituents.

These characteristics which are possessed of the three paths of being are of the nature of the manifested, when they exist in the present, and of the nature of the subtle when they passed into the past or are yet to be manifested.

परिणामैकत्वाद् वस्तुतत्त्वम्॥४.१४॥

pariṇāmaikatvād vastutattvam ॥4.14॥

4.14 The specificity of the object derives from the homogeneity of its transformation.

Vyāsa: When all are qualities, how is it that one emerges as sound and the other as sense? One modification of the qualities possessed of the nature of illumination, activity and inertia and being instrumentive appear in the shape of organs. Another modification of qualities appears in the objective state as the sound associated with the sound-tanmātra.

The earth-element is a modification of sound. Other elements take up the generic qualities smoothness, temperature, impulsion and space.

There is no object not co-existent with ideas. There are, however, ideas that are non-existent with objects.

Ideas belong to a plane of existence that goes beyond objects. This indicates that to see the world only as objects is incorrect.

वस्तुसाम्ये चित्तभेदात् तयोर्विभक्तः पन्थाः ॥४.१५॥

vastusāmye cittabhedāt tayorvibhaktaḥ panthāḥ ॥4.15॥

4.15 In view of the multiplicity of minds as opposed to the singleness of the object, the two belong to separate levels of existence.

That the same idea can produce a definite reaction amongst different minds is generally accepted. It cannot be said that the idea was imagined first by a single mind or imagined by more minds than one.

Ideas are able to elicit specific emotions in different people. Thus ideas are not to be taken to be the product of specific minds but rather having existence of their own. If ideas did not have existence of their own, different individuals could never speak of exactly the same idea.

If ideas have independent existence, they must be potentially available in some form to all individuals. This form must be intuitive which could be termed their *deep structure*.

This has the greatest implications for education. How should one be taught so that the individual is able to access the multitude of ideas within one's inner sky?

न चैकचित्ततन्त्रं चेद्वस्तु तत्प्रमाणकं तदा किं स्यात्॥४.१६॥

na caikacittatantraṃ cedvastu tatpramāṇakaṃ tadā kiṃ syāt ||4.16||

4.16 The object is not contingent on a single mind because if it were so what will happen when it is not cognized by the mind?

If any object (or idea) were dependent on a specific mind then when the mind was in saṃyama or performing some other activity it would not be cognized by any other mind.

Further, parts of the object that are not in touch with the mind will not exist. Thus objects are self-dependent and common to all sentient beings. Minds are also likewise self-dependent.

तदुपरागापेक्षत्वात् चित्तस्य वस्तु ज्ञाताज्ञातम्॥४.१७॥

taduparāgāpekṣatvāt cittasya vastu jñātājñātaṃ ||4.17||

4.17 An object is known or not known according to how it affects the mind.

Vyāsa: Objects are like magnets and the mind is like iron. Objects coming into contact with the mind color it. Whatever object colors the mind that objects become known. That which becomes known is an object. That which is thus not known is the Puruṣa. The mind is changeful as it assumes the natures of the known and unknown objects.

The mind has definite characteristics that define its properties. These characteristics represent universal characteristics of matter and to that extent they are of immense interest to ordinary science. The coloring of the mind by the object is a universal property. This property arises from fundamental laws of prakṛti.

सदा ज्ञाताश्चित्तवृत्तयस्तत्प्रभोः पुरुषस्यापरिणामित्वात्॥४.१८॥

sadājñātāścittavrttayastatprabhoḥ puruṣasyāpariṇāmitvāt ॥4.18॥

4.18 The fluctuations of the mind are always known by the superior, because of the immutability of the self.

Vyāsa: To the Puruṣa, whose sphere of functioning is the mind, mental modifications are ever known, because of its unchangeability. If the Puruṣa also changed like the mind, it would be impossible to determine its function.

Since beyond the mind exists the ground of consciousness, that ground must not be affected by time and, therefore, be able to know the fluctuations of the mind.

न तत् स्वाभासंदृश्यत्वात्॥४.१९॥

na tat svābhāsaṃdṛśyatvāt ॥4.19॥

4.19 That mind has no self-luminosity because of its character.

The idea that the mind is self-illuminating as well as illuminator of objects is dismissed by commentators. The analogy of the mind being like fire is not valid. If the mind were self-illuminating, it would not be perceivable by any other entity.

The mind cannot be self-illuminating because then it must be of two kinds, namely consciousness and object at the same time. When one naïvely speaks of the self-illumination of the mind, one is conflating several categories.

एकसमये चोभयानवधारणम्॥४.२०॥

ekasamaye cobhayānavadhāraṇam ॥4.20॥

4.20 This implies the impossibility of cognizing both the mind and the object simultaneously.

It is not possible that in one moment both one's own nature and the nature of other objects may be ascertained. The mind and the object are like the image (*bimba*) and its reflection (*pratibimba*). The image and the reflection have a causal relationship and they don't each exist independently.

चित्तान्तरदृश्ये बुद्धिबुद्धेरतिप्रसङ्गः स्मृतिसंकरश्च॥४.२१॥

cittāntaradṛśye buddhibuddheratiprasaṅgaḥ smṛtisaṃkaraśca ॥4.21॥

4.21 If consciousness were to be perceived by another consciousness that would lead to infinite regress from cognition to cognition and to a confusion to memory.

Consciousness cannot be in multiplicity because then we will not have *one universe*. Logic requires that consciousness be a unity and thus this most surprising basis of yoga and the Veda is compelled upon us also by the need for logical consistency.

चितेरप्रतिसंक्रमायास्तदाकारापत्तौ स्वबुद्धिसंवेदनम् ॥४.२२॥

citerapratisaṃkramāyāstadākārāpattau svabuddhi saṃvedanam ॥4.22॥

4.22 When the unchanging transcendental awareness assumes the shape of the mind, it leads to the experience of one's own cognitions.

Consciousness projects its own will by transforming its appearance, though not itself moving from place to place.

द्रष्टृदृश्योपरक्तं चित्तं सर्वार्थम् ॥४.२३॥

draṣṭṛdṛśyoparaktaṃ cittaṃ sarvārtham ॥4.23॥

4.23 Provided that consciousness is colored by the seer and the seen, it can perceive any object.

Vyāsa: The mind is colored by the objects of thought. The mind being itself an object comes into relationship with Puruṣa through its modifications as self. Thus it is said that the mind is colored by both subjectivity and objectivity, the knower and the knowable and it assumes the nature of both the conscious and the unconscious. Although it is of the nature of the objective, it appears as if it were of the nature of the subjective. Although it is devoid of consciousness by its nature, it appears as if it were consciousness.

It is by this similarity of mental appearance that some people are deceived into saying that the mind itself is the conscious agent. There are others who say that all this is but the mind and there is nothing in existence of the objective world.

Those who teach that the knower, the knowable, and the means of knowledge are the three modifications of the mind and thus divide the phenomena into three classes are the true philosophers.

तदसंख्येयवासनाभिः चित्तमपि परार्थं संहत्यकारित्वात्॥४.२४॥

tadasaṅkhyeyavāsanābhiḥ cittamapi parārtham saṃhatyakāritvāt ||4.24||

4.24 That [the mind] though filled by countless latent impressions exists for another since it acts conjointly.

Vyāsa: The mind is colored by innumerable residua and so it must exist for another.

As a house which has assumed its shape by various materials being brought together cannot come into existence for itself, so also the mind assumes its function and shape by many things coming together. The mental phenomenon of pleasure cannot exist for its own sake and nor does knowledge exist for itself. Both these exist for the sake of another, who is Puruṣa.

विशेषदर्शिन आत्मभावभावनाविनिवृत्तिः॥४.२५॥

viśeṣadarśinaḥ ātmabhāvabhāvanāvinivṛttiḥ ||4.25||

4.25 For him who sees the distinction comes the cessation of the feeling of [the false] self-sense.

Vyāsa: As the existence of seeds is inferred from blades of grass shooting forth in the rainy season, so it is inferred that he whose tears flow and whose hair stand on end when he hears of the path of liberation has a store of karma tending to liberation. The curiosity about the nature of the self is naturally manifested in him.

The curiosity about the nature of the self appears as the questions:

Who was I?
How was I?
What is this?
How is this?
What shall we become?
How shall we become?

These questions disappear in one who sees the distinction between the mind and the Puruṣa. The change affects the mind alone.

The curiosity in the absence of avidyā is pure and untouched by the characteristics of the mind. Counterintuitively, the curiosity regarding the nature of the self ceases for the wise.

तदा विवेकनिम्नं कैवल्यप्राग्भारं चित्तम्॥४.२६॥

tadā vivekanimnaṃ kaivalyaprāgbhāraṃ cittam ॥4.26॥

4.26 Then the mind is inclined towards discernment and is borne towards independence.

The mind that was absorbed in sensory pleasures and materiality takes a different path. It is now borne towards independence and discriminative knowledge.

तच्छिद्रेषु प्रत्ययान्तराणि संस्कारेभ्यः॥४.२७॥

tacchidreṣu pratyayāntarāṇi saṃskārebhyaḥ ॥4.27॥

4.27 At intervals other ideas may arise from the saṃskāras.

It is not that one is established in the state of discriminative knowledge at all times. One normally cycles through a series of states during the day that are triggered by force of habit, associations with places and persons, and by karmic chain of events.

हानम् एषां क्लेशवदुक्तम्॥४.२८॥

Hānam eṣāṃ kleśavaduktam ॥4.28॥

4.28 Their cessation is by the same means as for hindrances.

It is through practice that such lapses become less troublesome. The practice *wakes* one up from the *automatic* behavior of our daily lives.

प्रसंख्यानेऽप्यकुसीदस्य सर्वथाविवेकख्यातेर्धर्ममेघः समाधिः॥४.२९॥

prasaṃkhyāne'pyakusīdasya sarvathāvivekakhyāterdharmameghaḥ samādhiḥ ॥4.29॥

4.29 For one who is detached even for this mastery, there follows, through a vision of discernment, concentration called the Cloud-of-Virtue.

When the practitioner has no attachment left for the highest intellection, he gets into a state called the Cloud-of-Virtue. This state is a mode where one has broken free from one's normal moods and is in an elevated state of goodness.

ततः क्लेशकर्मनिवृत्तिः ॥४.३०॥

tataḥ kleśakarmanivṛttiḥ ॥4.30॥

4.30 Thence follows the cessation of the hindrances and of karma.

After the saṃskāras leading to the good and bad actions have been uprooted and the afflictions are gone, the wise man becomes free even when alive (*jīvanamukta*).

The *jīvanamukta* is attached to higher purpose and the universal. Since his actions are not motivated by personal greed, he remains unaffected by their consequences.

तदा सर्वावरणमलापेतस्य ज्ञानस्याऽनन्त्याज्ज्ञेयम् अल्पम् ॥४.३१॥

tadā sarvāvaraṇamalāpetasya jñānasyā'nantyājjñeyam alpam ॥4.31॥

4.31 Then, with all coverings of imperfection removed, little remains to be known because of the infinitude of the resulting knowledge.

Knowledge when rid of the impurities of affliction and action become infinite. When knowledge becomes infinite, little remains to be known. Of this state it has been said: "The blind man pierced the pearl, the fingerless put a thread into it, the neckless wore it, and the tongueless praised it." Such a state of knowledge makes it possible to bridge paradoxes of ordinary awareness.

ततः कृतार्थानां परिणामक्रमसमाप्तिर्गुणानाम् ॥४.३२॥

tataḥ kṛtārthānāṃ pariṇāmakramasamāptirguṇānām ॥4.32॥

4.32 Thence ceases the sequence of mutations of primary constituents, their purpose being realized.

In the state of knowledge, there is perfect harmony amongst the guṇas. It is like the state of perfect entropy which remains unchanged by further evolution.

क्षणप्रतियोगी परिणामापरान्त निर्ग्राह्यः क्रमः ॥४.३३॥

kṣaṇapratiyogī pariṇāmāparānta nirgrāhyaḥ kramaḥ ॥4.33॥

4.33 The positive people correlate to the moment, recognized as such at the terminal point of the moment, in a sequence.

Succession is found in the permanent also. This permanence is two-fold: the eternal in perfection, and the eternal in evolution. Of these, the perfect eternity belongs to Puruṣa. The evolutionary eternity belongs to the qualities. The eternal is that in which the substance is not destroyed by changing appearances. Both are permanent since their substance is never destroyed.

Vyāsa asks the old question again: *Is it that all that is born must die and having been dead be born again?*

He in whom the light of knowledge has appeared, and whose desires have been destroyed, that wise man is not born again; the rest are reborn. The wise man who is not born again is due to the fact that he is part of the larger unfolding world.

पुरुषार्थशून्यानां गुणानां प्रतिप्रसवः कैवल्यं, स्वरूपप्रतिष्ठा वा चितिशक्तिरेति ॥४.३४॥

puruṣārthaśūnyānāṃ guṇānāṃ-pratiprasavaḥ kaivalyaṃ svarūpapratiṣṭhā vā citiśaktireti ॥4.34॥

4.34 *Freedom (aloneness) is the inverse generation of the primary constituents, devoid of purpose for the self, or it is the establishment of the power of awareness in its own form.*

Freedom and aloneness are two sides of the same coin. When one is totally free, one is also alone. But it is not the aloneness of the isolated person. Rather, it is being one with the only single entity that pervades the universe, namely, consciousness.

Absolute freedom comes when the succession of the functioning of the qualities in the performance of their duties is over. Absolute freedom is the latency of the qualities on becoming devoid of the object of the Puruṣa, or it is the power of consciousness established in its own nature.

इति पतञ्जलिविरचिते योगसूत्रे चतुर्थः कैवल्यपादः।

Here ends the fourth part of Patañjali's Yoga-sūtra on the freedom.

॥इति पातञ्जलयोगसूत्राणि॥

Here ends the Patañjali's Yoga-sūtra.

Epilogue

Patañjali's Yoga-sūtra provides a plan for starting on the exploration of the labyrinth of the mind. For someone interested primarily in the āsanas, it gives the larger context as the āsanas were known to Vyāsa, the early commentator on the sūtras. The āsanas are an integral part of the eight-step ladder of Patañjali's yoga. They are one step in the exploration of the mind. The connections between the mind and the body are apparent to any thoughtful person and, therefore, sooner or later the āsana practitioner wishes to further the exploration beyond the body.

The Yoga-Sūtra first teaches the individual to have ethical principles and study oneself and have passion for knowing oneself. As the practitioner deepens the practice, he learns to make a distinction between his essential self and the habits he has acquired.

He learns first to recognize what aspects of his behavior are good and bad saṃskāras, learnt latent impressions and habits of mind. Once he has obtained this discrimination, he learns how to use his saṃskāras to obtain new insights and finally transcend the saṃskāras also to obtain extraordinary wisdom. This also puts him in touch with capacities he scarcely knew existed within him. This shows the practitioner how to tap the infinite potential and creativity that resides within him so that he is free. It teaches him to attain equanimity, overcome fear and suffering, and have love for all beings.

The yogi is a person of sensitivity and compassion. He lives to the fullest. But he is like the swan who, while living on the water, remains dry. For the yogi, the present is of the utmost significance and each interaction is important. He does not carry grudges or resentments and he does not live in the past although he acknowledges it fully. He does not belittle others and he approaches all interactions with positivity. He is not afraid of the future.

The yogi begins by recognizing that he needs to master his mind and transcend its function. Having done so, the mind truly becomes an instrument and not the master of his actions. If the mind is the monkey, the yogi's practices make it possible for him to fully train this monkey.

The individual who is not on a path of freedom is likely to be driven by passion, greed, or feelings of anger and resentment. If we are born free, we are put in bondage by upbringing and culture. The nature of this bondage varies from one society to another. It is clear of course that certain societies and culture, who have found it harder to break from their collective saṃskāras, treat their people badly or have a high degree of violence. In some there is violence against women; others believe that only people of their faith or ethnicity should have political rights.

We should also not believe that people in other societies cannot find redemption and freedom. The breath of the eternal has touched everyone at some point or other in their lives. A person will be set on the path of self-study and understanding if he is encouraged to leverage his acknowledged virtues and find brotherhood in all mankind and in all life.

The yogi learns that his inner world mirrors the universe. There are within him both the forces of light and that of darkness, of transcendence and materiality. These two opposite forces are like the two wings of the bird both of which should flap for him to be able to fly. He cannot try to deny any of these but rather put them to use in a fashion that both these aspects help him along in his path. It is through a churning within the ocean of his self that he can obtain uncommon understanding and intuition.

Several sets of complementary opposites constitute the yogi's inner world as they do of any other individual. But since the yogi is the master of the house of his mind, he can keep the forces of materiality in check.

The practice of the yogi transforms and liberates him. This represents the *mukti* or freedom or *nirvāṇa* or extinction. He is not bound by habits of mind and burdened by explicit and implicit memories. Since his actions are free, they are imbued with creative intelligence, and he is liberated from the chain of instinctual action and reaction, which is the law of karma.

But yoga is not just a set of practices to make a person deal with life's challenges and vicissitudes. It provides answers to the deepest questions of the nature of reality and of life. These answers are not in terms of faith or belief in an ideological system but rather in terms of a heartfelt recognition of one's connection to the larger fabric of life. The individual becomes a scientist whose intuition helps him find new vistas and in the process his intuition is also deepened.

Yoga is not just about individual's freedom. It also applies to society. Just like the individual, the collective society should exercise its *yamas* and *niyamas*, that is have ethical principles and not serve just one group or another at the exclusion of others, and strive to separate its immediate self-interest from a larger good that applies to all humanity.

It is not true that societies that are materially more advanced ensure better all-round development of its citizens. There may be more political freedom but this freedom is notional and symbolic in many arenas. There is unethical treatment of animals in beef, pig, and chicken farms and most people are not even aware of the terrible conditions in the food industry.

Modern advanced societies are also lacking in inculcating simple living, attachment to knowledge and philosophy, and purity of action. The educational system does not encourage svādhyāya, or self-study.

Instead of practices that develop concentration and meditation, television and movies provide escapist entertainment. Instead of the ecstasy of samādhi, people are opting for drug and alcohol induced highs which alternate with episodes of depression and dependence on medication.

The wisdom of yoga as given in the Bhagavad Gītā and Patañjali's Yoga-sūtra is of great relevance to our times for a variety of reasons. It not only provides us insights to help find our latent creativity but also gives us extraordinary understanding of reality and our role in the world. Man in the developed world may live in unprecedented luxury, but he also faces unprecedented challenges. Technology has alienated him from nature. Schoolbooks, media, political parties, and corporations are encouraging values of consumption and instant sense gratification.

Yoga practice should not be seen merely as a means to provide health, community and compassion for all creatures. While all those are laudable ends, the fundamental purpose of yoga is to intuitively understand the nature of reality and man's place in it.

The basis of modern society is man's material nature and it is filling people up with depression and deep unhappiness. People are increasingly addicted or dependent on medication, drugs, alcohol, and empty entertainment and they are becoming self-absorbed with little interest in their fellow beings. Yoga, on the other hand, advocates engagement with the world at many different levels. Maha Upaniṣad 6.72 declares *vasudhaiva kuṭumbakam*, the world is a family.

The practice of yoga means different things depending on the stage of the practice. For some, it is just āsanas and the aesthetic of physical form. At another level, it is the training of the mind and finding bliss in the aesthetics of beauty. At yet another level, it is to know the secret of consciousness and take delight in its play in the world.

Notes

For translations from the commentaries of Vyāsa and Vācaspati Miśra, I have depended mainly on the book by Prasāda (1912/1982); the Yogavārttika of Vijñānabhikṣu is described by Rukmani (1981). The translations from the Yoga-Vāsiṣṭha are based on the book by Venkatesananda (1993). For more recent translations on general material on yoga, see Feuerstein (2008), and Bryant (2009). Feuerstein (2008) presents excerpts from a variety of sources. Frawley (2000) and Frawley (2008) deal with the roots of yoga in the Vedas. The notes below cover the various sections of the Introduction.

I. *Mind's Construction of Reality.* My father's autobiography (R.N. Kak, 1995) describes his yogic apprenticeship. There is overwhelming evidence that supports the yogic view that the mind constructs reality. This is seen most clearly in patients with brain injuries (Gazzaniga, 1995; Sacks, 1985). The autobiography of Gopi Krishna (1970) proposes that there ought to be neurophysiological changes in the brain of a yogi.

An account of the life of Lalleśvarī is in J. Kak (2007); medical experiments on Swami Rama are given in Boyd (2007); Svātmārāma's Haṭha Yoga Pradīpikā (Saraswati, 1985) presents a detailed account of the cakras.

René Descartes' (1596-1650) declaration that animals don't have thought and reason came to influence Western thought for a long time. Decartes wrote that "[A]fter the error of those who deny God, there is none that leads weak minds further from the straight path of virtue than that of imagining that the souls of beasts are of the same nature as our own" (Descartes, 1637/1988). He said the animals did no have thought since they did not have language and they had no reason since they were incapable of communicating their learnt knowledge to other animals. Modern research on animal behavior negaes both these arguments. The long-standing influence of Descartes was due to his view being in agreement with the Christian belief that humans were central to God's creation on earth.

In opposition to Descartes, the eighteenth century philosopher David Hume (1711-1776) asserted in his *A Treastise of Human Nature* that "no truth appears to be more evident, than that beasts are endow'd with thought and reason as well as men." He explained that since animal behavior was very similar to human behavior, it stands to reason that both animals and humans form associations in the mind in a similar fashion (Hume, 1739/1978).

It has been argued that there are intuitively compelling grounds for believing that many animals have conscious beliefs and desires as well as sophisticated emotions (Roberts, 2009; Lurz, 2011). People with pets have no difficulty agreeing with this view.

Griffin (1984, 2001) and Griffin and Speck (2007) present summary of the evidence that animals are conscious the same way as humans.

The mapping of distributed brain processes to behavior and cognition must include the influence of social context and history that also go towards generating the subjective feel of the world. The neurophysiological component of this equation is provided by activity in the neural circuity of the brain and in the functional modules that map to specific conscious states. The mapping is further complicated by the self-organization of the brain since activity and behavior have implications for structure. This indicates that the idea of mind/brain identity based on a classical computational framework is incorrect, which is consistent with the finding that there is no unified neural correlate of consciousness (Zeki, 2003).

But if there is no single neural correlate, how do distributed lower-level consciousnesses relate to each other, and how does the integration of the neural activity take place? The general view is that the communication between preconscious states somehow maps to a single consciousness although the conceptual framework in which the communication may be addressed is not defined.

One can speak of a model of different hierarchically defined consciousnesses states that are mediated by languages and metalanguages with varying capacity or ability to recruit lower level consciousness states. Some of the languages are certain to be quantum in character. The highest node in this hierarchical model, which is located in a non-physical space, represents the unitary consciousness but it does not have a single neural correlate, and, in this sense, it agrees with the available evidence.

II. *Outer and Inner Skies.* For further discussion of the connections between the inner and the outer, see Kak (2007), Kak (2009) and Kak (2010). These connections are called *bandhu* in the Vedic texts. The quotation by Ramaṇa Maharṣi is from the book by Venkatesananda (1993).

III. *Patañjali and his Times.* Aklujkar (1997) presents the evidence on Patañjali's origins. The problem of the three texts attributed to Patañjali is discussed in most books on Indian philosophy such as Radhakrishnan (1940) and Dasgupta (1955).

IV. *Paradoxical Knowledge and the Veda.* See Kak (2000) and Feuerstein et al (1995) for general information. The significant fact about Vedic books is that they claim to address the mystery of consciousness; see also Kak, (1986) and Kak (2004) for a general review of the problem.

V. *Light and Time.* The Vaiśeṣika sūtras provide us the most ancient systematic exposition of matter in terms of atomic structure. Unlike Greek physics, the Vaiśeṣika sūtras do not deal only with substances but also the sentient observer.

VI. *The Saṃskāra Theory.* The theory of saṃskāras is a natural component of the Indian approach to mind and consciousness. The books by Dasgupta (1955), Raju (1971), and Radhakrishnan (1940) present a summary of Indian psychology.

VII. *Yoga of the Bhagavad Gītā.* See Aurobindo (2000), Miller (1986), and Feuerstein (2005).

VIII. *Vāsiṣṭha's Yoga.* The Yoga Vāsiṣṭha is available in English in an abridged translation by Swami Venkatesananda (1993).

IX. *Tantra and Śrī Vidyā.* We wish to show in this section that tantra's origins are much earlier than has hitherto been supposed (Kak, 2008/2009).

X. *The Sri Cakra and Lalitā Tripurasundarī.* Subramaniam (1977) and Vrajavallabhadvivedaḥ (1988); also see Goudriaan and Gupta (1981). For a Sri Cakra basis to the design of the Prambanan temple, see Kak (2011).

XI. *The Vijñānabhairava.* See Singh (1979) and Vrajavallabhadvivedaḥ (1988). For Kashmir Śaivism in its historical development, see Abhinavagupta (2005), and J. Singh (1979).

XII. *Cognitive Abilities.* See Gazzaniga (1995) and Sacks (1985) for a general review. For details on the musical abilities of Thomas Wiggins, see O'Connell (2009). William James spoke of two kinds of selves: the self as knower (the "I"), and the self as known (the "me"). Each person's self is partly subjective (as knower) and partly objective (as known). The objective self itself may be described in its three aspects: the material self, the social self, and the spiritual self (James, 1890).

Bibliography

Abhinavagupta (2005). Parātrīśikā Vivaraṇa. Delhi.

Aklujkar, A. (1997). Kashmir and Patañjali's Mahābhāṣya. Xth World Sanskrit Conference, 3-9 January, Bangalore.

Aurobindo, S. (2000). Essays on the Gita. Pondicherry.

Boyd, D. (2007). Swami: Encounters with Modern Mystics. New York.

Bryant, E.F. (2009). The Yoga Sūtras of Patañjali. New York.

Dasgupta, S. (1955). A History of Indian Philosophy. Cambridge.

Descartes, R. (1637/1988). Discourse on the Method. In Cottingham, Stoothoff, and Murdoch (Trans.) Descartes: Selected Philosophical Writings. Cambridge.

Feuerstein, G. (2008). The Yoga Tradition. Prescott.

Feuerstein, G., Kak, S., Frawley, D. (1995). In Search of the Cradle of Civilization. Wheaton.

Frawley, D. (2000). Vedantic Meditation. New York.

Frawley, D. (2008). Yoga, the Greater Tradition. San Rafael.

Gazzaniga, M.S. (1995). The Cognitive Neurosciences. Cambridge.

Goudriaan, T. and Gupta, S. (1981). Hindu Tantric and Śākta Literature. Wiesbaden.

Griffin, D.R. (1984). Animal Thinking. Cambridge, MA.

Griffin, D. (2001). Animal Minds: Beyond Cognition to Consciousness. Chicago.

Griffin, D. & Speck, G. (2007). New Evidence of Animal Consciousness. Animal Cognition 7:5-18.

Hume, D. (1739/1978). A Treatise of Human Nature. Edited by P. H. Nidditch, 2nd Ed. Oxford.

James, W. (1890/1999). The Principles of Psychology. New York. Reprinted 1999, Bristol.

Kak, J. (2007). Mystical Verses of Lallā. Delhi.

Kak, R.N. (1995). Autumn Leaves: Kashmiri Reminiscences. New Delhi.

Kak, S. (1986, 2016). The Nature of Physical Reality. Mississauga.

Kak, S. (2002). The Gods Within. New Delhi.

Kak, S. (2004). The Architecture of Knowledge. Delhi.

Kak, S. (2007). The Prajñā Sūtras: Aphorisms of Intuition. New Delhi.

Kak, S. (2015). The Wishing Tree. New Delhi.

Kak, S. (2008/2009). The Great Goddess Lalitā and the Śrī Cakra. Brahmavidyā: The Adyar Library Bulletin, vol. 72-73, pp. 155-172.

Kak, S. (2009). The universe, quantum physics, and consciousness. Journal of Cosmology 3: 500-510.

Kak, S. (2010). Visions of the cosmos. Journal of Cosmology 9: 2063-2077.

Kak, S. (2011). Space and order in Prambanan. In Manju Shree (ed.), From Beyond The Eastern Horizon: Essays In Honour Of Professor Lokesh Chandra. Delhi.

Krishna, G. (1971). Kundalini: the Evolutionary Energy in Man. Boulder.

Lurz, R. (2011). Mindreading Animals: The Debate over What Animals Know about Other Minds. Cambridge, MA.

Miller, B.S. (1986). The Bhagavad-Gita: Krishna's Counsel in Time of War, New York.

O'Connell, D. (2009). The Ballad of Blind Tom: Slave Pianist. New York.

Prasāda, R. (1912/1982). Patanjali's Yoga Sutras. Allahabad/New Delhi.

Radhakrishnan, S. (1940). Indian Philosophy, Vols. I, II. London.

Raju, P.T. (1971). The Philosophical Traditions of India. London.

Roberts, R. (2009). The sophistication of non-human emotion. In R. Lurz (Ed.) The Philosophy of Animal Minds. Cambridge.

Rukmani, T.S. (1981). Yogavārttika of Vijñānabhikṣu. Delhi.

Sacks, O. (1985). The Man Who Mistook His Wife for a Hat. New York.

Saraswati, S. (1985). Hatha Yoga Pradipika. Munger.

Schrödinger, E. (1959). Mind and Matter. Cambridge.

Schrödinger, E. (1965). What is Life? New York.

Singh, J. (1979). Vijñānabhairava. Delhi.

Subramaniam, V.K. (1977). Saundaryalaharī. Delhi.

Venkatesananda, Swami (1993). Vasiṣṭha's Yoga. Albany.

Vrajavallabhadvivedaḥ (1988). Yoginīhṛdayam. Delhi.

Zeki, S. (2003). The disunity of consciousness.Trends Cogn. Sci. 7: 214–218.

Index

Made in the USA
Monee, IL
21 February 2022

91592551R00075